gy

Jo   Thompson

D1332563

F BOOKS

For UK order queries: please contact Bookpoint Ltd, 39 Milton Park, Abingdon, Oxon OX14 4TD. Telephone: (44) 01235 400414, Fax: (44) 01235 400454. Lines are open from 9.00–6.00, Monday to Saturday, with a 24 hour message answering service. Email address: orders@bookpoint.co.uk

For U.S.A. & Canada order queries: please contact NTC/Contemporary Publishing, 4255 West Touhy Avenue, Lincolnwood, Illinois 60646–1975, U.S.A. Telephone: (847) 679 5500, Fax: (847) 679 2494.

Long renowned as the authoritative source for self-guided learning – with more than 30 million copies sold worldwide – the *Teach Yourself* series includes over 200 titles in the fields of languages, crafts, hobbies, sports, and other leisure activities.

A catalogue entry for this title is available from The British Library.

Library of Congress Catalog Card Number: 98-67261

First published in UK 1998 by Hodder Headline Plc, 338 Euston Road, London, NW1 3BH.

First published in US 1998 by NTC/Contemporary Publishing, 4255 West Touhy Avenue, Lincolnwood (Chicago), Illinois 60646–1975 U.S.A.

Cover photo from The Stock Market

Typeset by Transet Limited, Coventry, England.
Printed in Great Britain for Hodder & Stoughton Educational, a division of Hodder Headline Plc, 338 Euston Road, London NW1 3BH by Cox & Wyman Ltd, Reading, Berkshire.

Impression number   10 9 8 7 6 5 4 3 2 1
Year   2002 2001 2000 1999 1998

To Tim Cloudsley
Social Scientist and Ecologist

Acknowledgements

My warmest thanks are due to David Applin who kindly read the first draft and made many valuable suggestions; to Peter Marshall for useful advice regarding Appendix C; to Joanne Osborn of Hodder & Stoughton for her encouragement and understanding; to Eileen Bergh for typing the manuscript; and, as always, to my dearest wife Anne Cloudsley.

CONTENTS

1 | WHAT IS ECOLOGY?

Ecology is the study of the interrelationships between living organisms and their environments, both inorganic and organic. The inorganic environment consists of the atmosphere, light, water, inorganic salts, soils and so on. All these factors are interrelated. The primeval atmosphere of the Earth, when life began, was very different from the air of today. It contained many gases that are injurious to life and there was no free oxygen because plants had not yet evolved. No matter how life on Earth first arose it would, almost certainly, never begin again in exactly the same way if it were exterminated.

Soils, as we shall see, not only influence the distribution of plants and animals but are created by them. Add to this the fluctuating and ever changing interactions between plants, fungi, animals, viruses, bacteria and so on, and you will readily understand that ecology is a very complex subject indeed.

The word **ecology** was first used by E.H. Haeckel in 1869 (as the German *ökologie*) from the Greek *oikos* or 'house' and *logos*, which means 'discourse'. It can be defined as: the scientific study of the relationships that exist among organisms as well as between organisms and all aspects, living and non-living, of their environments.

We study ecology for a number of reasons. First and, to my mind, foremost because it is interesting. Human beings gain intellectual satisfaction from understanding natural patterns and processes. If this were not so, who would bother to gaze at the stars through a telescope? Most of the major benefits of science to humanity have been accidental, in the sense that they were 'spin-offs' from basic research carried out, in the first instance, mainly for the sake of curiosity. The emphasis placed on the practical applications of ecological knowledge is understandable, but it reflects only one aspect of its importance and fascination.

The fitness of the environment

The world in which we live is little more than a lump of rock orbiting the Sun. On, or near, its surface are many different living organisms, all of which, ultimately, depend upon the Sun's nuclear energy. Some of this energy reaches the Earth in the form of sunlight. Green plants convert the energy of sunlight into chemical energy. Without plants and their ability to produce foods that store chemical energy, there would be no animals. A few bacteria may be able to live in deep caverns, sulphur lakes, hydrothermal vents at the bottom of the ocean deeps and other surprising environments, but they may well not have evolved there in the first instance – although not everyone agrees about this.

Photosynthesis

Green plants form **carbohydrates** by **photosynthesis** (named from the Greek words meaning 'light' and 'build'). Carbon dioxide gas and water first combine to form the sugar glucose. Oxygen is produced as a waste product. Carbohydrates contain the elements carbon, hydrogen and oxygen. Examples are provided by sugars, starch and cellulose. Plants also synthesise **amino acids**, which contain nitrogen in addition to the elements found in carbohydrates. Animals breathe in oxygen and feed on the carbohydrates and amino acids that are produced by plants. Because they prey upon other animals that feed upon plants, even carnivorous animals are dependent upon vegetable matter.

Both plants and animals use amino acids to synthesise or build up even more complicated chemical substances, such as **proteins**. They also convert carbohydrates into fats. The bodies of animals consist mainly of water, carbohydrates, proteins and fats. Their waste products and their bodies, after they die, provide much of the nitrogen that plants use to synthesise amino acids. So, in their turn, plants are dependent, to a degree, upon animals. Moreover, the carbon dioxide that animals produce is used by plants although very much more comes from volcanoes and other geological sources.

Requirements for life

All living organisms require atmospheric gases, water, chemical nutrients, space and the opportunity to reproduce themselves. However, these are not distributed evenly and, consequently, living organisms are not distributed uniformly either. Nutritional resources also vary greatly in quality as well as in quantity. There are, therefore, great evolutionary pressures towards specialisation in requirements. These pressures derive from competition between individuals and from the variable nature of the environment. They result in the profusion of living species seen on Earth today. (For an explanation of species, see Appendix I, *Classification of living organisms*.)

In 1913, L.J. Henderson published a book *The Fitness of the Environment* which is, today, almost forgotten. In this book, he pointed out that the physical properties of the environment present a unique collection of properties that are essential for the maintenance of life. These properties cover different systems, from the special properties of carbon and of water to the specific conditions which made life possible on Earth. For example, water is the only liquid that changes its state from solid (ice) to gas (vapour) within a range of temperatures so restricted that they do not cause the breakdown of biochemical compounds, themselves dependent upon the unique ability of carbon to form loose addition compounds with other elements. For instance, when we breathe, the haemoglobin in our blood takes up oxygen from the air and gives off carbon dioxide. The oxygen is bound in a loose, easily reversible manner.

On the other hand it can be argued that, in general, the cosmic environment is extremely unfit to support life. The fact that water requires much more heat than metal or rock to raise its temperature makes the temperature of the Earth remarkably stable because it is largely covered by deep oceans. A planet with a more variable temperature would be less suitable for life but, if a broader range of temperatures were experienced over a long period of time, there is little doubt that life would have adapted to it. Nevertheless, this range would be very limited in comparison with that between absolute zero and the temperature in the interior of the Sun. Some sulphur-metabolising bacteria do, however, thrive in deep-sea hydrothermal vents at temperatures of 110 °C or more, while certain marine algae manage to survive in pockets of saturated brine at –18 °C!

Autecology and synecology

Complex problems, like jigsaw puzzles, have to be solved piece by piece. Ecology involves a number of interactive disciplines. **Autecology** is the ecology of individual organisms or species. It includes physiological ecology, **ethology** (or animal behaviour) and population dynamics.

Synecology is the study of entire plant and animal communities, including **ecosystems**. This term was coined in 1935 by A.G. Tansley to describe a natural unit consisting of living and non-living components that interact to form a stable system.

Synecology is much more complex than autecology because so many variable factors are involved. It often requires complex mathematical analysis of data and, because of this, most naturalists and amateur biologists, as well as many professionals, tend to study autecological problems. For instance, they may investigate the distribution of a plant species and the influence of soil and climate upon it; or they might question how food supply affects the numbers of eggs laid by a particular species of bird. An autecological problem of immense environmental and economic importance concerns the spread of the South American water hyacinth (*Eichornia crassipes*) throughout the waterways of Central Africa and elsewhere. If it were known what regulates the plant's populations in its natural home, biological control measures incorporating this knowledge could be introduced to control what has become a serious pest in other tropical regions to which it has been introduced.

In recent years, it has become clear that, at the highest level of complexity of organisation, the **community**, plants and animals are inseparably linked along with various environmental factors such as climate and soils, to form ecosystems. The world is divided into a number of geographic regions or **biomes**, each of which contains a varying number of ecosystems. Thus the **biosphere** – that portion of the Earth which supports life – heads a hierarchy of ecological units related to one another both in space and in the sequence of time.

The Gaia hypothesis

Gaia was an Earth goddess of the ancient Greeks. What we know as the Gaia hypothesis was formulated in the late 1960s when its principal author, James Lovelock, was working for the United States Space Agency (NASA). It states that, for most practical purposes, the Earth may be regarded as a single living organism and its inhabitants – viruses, bacteria, protistans, fungi, plants and animals – can be likened to the organs of an animal's body. In other words, the Earth is not an inanimate habitat for life but is a single, self-organising, living organism. Its surface should not be regarded as the environment of life, but as part of life itself.

The great advantage of this approach for non-scientists is that it helps them to appreciate the complexity of the environment in which we live and the harm that is currently being inflicted upon it by many human activities. Ecologists, however, tend to find the hypothesis unnecessary. To many of them, Gaia is little more than synecology invested with mysticism – and mysticism falls outside the realm of science. It is not part of ecology.

Yet, to be fair, it should be remembered that science does not pretend to embrace the entire spectrum of human knowledge and experience. Not all facts, however important or well established, come within its sphere. Science is limited to the consideration of those phenomena that are capable of being verified by any physically fit person possessing the necessary time, apparatus and technical skill. Furthermore, it depends upon various assumptions or presuppositions which are not themselves capable of rational proof, although they are usually regarded as self-evident. For instance, we presume that an event which always takes place, such as the daily rising and setting of the Sun, will continue into the distant future. Alternatively, if we mislay something in the house we naturally assume that it must still be somewhere there and has not vanished completely. We also expect natural phenomena to be ordered and rational because they normally are. Within the limits of the uncertainty principle in physics, chaos theory (see below) and experimental error, a well-designed experiment should always give the same results.

At the same time, analogies such as that likening the Earth to a single living organism can be both helpful and misleading. Charles Darwin's theory of natural selection or the 'survival of the fittest' depends to a considerable extent upon an analogy between the controlled breeding of domesticated plants and animals and the historical development of the organic world. The concept of Gaia or Mother Earth is romantic, poetic and useful, in that it encourages people to respect and care for the world around them, but it does not help ecologists to quantify and understand the balance of nature.

Chaos theory

A central controversy among ecologists in the early 1970s dealt with the very nature of population fluctuations. As we shall see later in this book, zoologists do not doubt that, in general, animal populations are regulated by environmental factors. With sufficient knowledge both of these and of the reproductive physiology of the species concerned, they assumed that population fluctuations could theoretically be predicted quite precisely. To test this assumption, an Australian scientist, Robert May, carried out a detailed mathematical exploration of the theoretical growth of a population of animals. Somewhat to his surprise, he found that, after a critical level had been reached, simple deterministic models produced random chaotic oscillations.

In this context, **chaos** can be defined as erratic changes in the sizes of populations governed by differential equations and having high intrinsic rates of growth. Chaos is not confined to mathematical theory, however. It is actually found in nature. It is well known, for instance, that human epidemic diseases strike the population in cycles, both regular and irregular. A programme of inoculation does not necessarily result in a steady reduction in the rate of infections. On the contrary, during the campaign to eradicate rubella or German measles from Britain, the general downward trend in the number of cases reported was sometimes interrupted by enormous oscillations. Although unexpected, these were quite in accordance with May's theoretical calculations.

Further evidence for the chaos theory comes from the records of measles epidemics in New York City, of chicken pox in the British Isles and in fluctuations of Canadian lynx populations as recorded over the years by trappers of the Hudson's Bay Company. In fact, chaos is evident in many aspects of the natural world – from the shapes of snowflakes, all of which are different, to the long-term forecasting of weather. In all of these, there is an incredibly delicate balance between the forces of stability and those of instability. The same is true in some fields of biology which, by its very nature, is an inexact science when compared with chemistry and physics. Another example is provided in the study of rhythms, the interplay between which may produce a special kind of chaos.

Fields of study

The approaches of biologists to the subject of ecology are diverse, and not all are discussed in this book. To learn more about genetic, behavioural and evolutionary ecology, environmental issues or cosmology, the reader is recommended to consult other volumes in the present series. Here we shall be concerned with energy flow, climates and soils, the biomes of the biosphere, populations and their regulation, ecosystems, habitats, predators and parasites, concluding with a consideration of the influence of human activities on the environment and on the diversity of species within it. Methods by which these topics can be investigated will be mentioned, in passing, and an attempt made to unite diverse approaches from theoretical ecology and empirical research in systems ranging from the inhabitants of soils to those of deserts, snowlands and ocean depths.

2 | ENERGY FLOW AND NUTRIENT CYCLES

As we have seen, the energy on which life depends comes from sunlight. This is used to convert carbon dioxide and water into carbohydrates through **photosynthesis**. Photosynthesis takes place in the presence of **chlorophyll**, the green pigment that gives plants their colour. Chlorophyll acts as a **catalyst** – an agent which engenders a chemical effect without itself taking part in the reaction. The basic chemical formula for the reaction is:

$$6CO_2 + 6H_2O \rightarrow C_6 H_{12} O_6 \text{ (glucose)} + 6O_2$$

Energy flow

The energy trapped by plants from the light of the Sun is released by the animals that feed on those plants. So energy can be said to flow through one organism into another as nutrients are cycled and recycled. One of the strongest proponents of this approach has been Eugene P. Odum, who described it in his book *Fundamentals of Ecology*, first published in 1953.

Odum depicted ecosystems as simple energy flow diagrams (Figure 2.1). Every living organism ingests energy. Some of this is used for respiration or growth, some is stored in the form of fat for future utilisation and some is not used at all. Plants themselves need energy for growth and reproduction. They also use energy to synthesise proteins. For this, they break down or **metabolise** the carbohydrates that they, themselves, have photosynthesised. The formula for the metabolism of glucose, for instance is:

$$C_6 H_{12} O_6 + 6 O_2 \rightarrow 6 CO_2 + 6 H_2O + \text{energy}$$

In his simple diagrams, Odum showed a box to represent the **biomass** (or its energy equivalent) of any organism or community. (Biomass is the mass of a living organism, or a number of organisms. The word is usually applied to the total mass of a species or group of organisms present in a

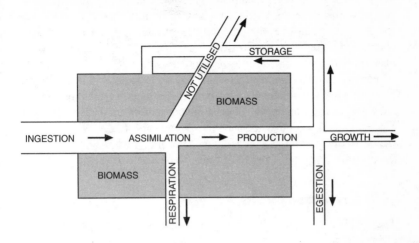

2.1 Energy flow (modified after E.P. Odum).

particular habitat or trophic level in a food chain: see below.) Feeding relationships linked energy flow diagrams into a food web. Energy flow diagrams were elaborated to illustrate the cycling of elements such as carbon, nitrogen and soil nutrients.

Producers, consumers and decomposers

Living organisms differ fundamentally in their modes of nutrition. Some, including many bacteria, obtain their energy from simple chemical reactions such as the reduction of sulphates in the formation of non-volcanic deposits of sulphur. They are known as **autotrophs**. Green plants are also autotrophs because they make use of light as a source of energy to synthesise carbohydrates. Autotrophs provide food for all other organisms and are therefore known as **producers**. The organisms that utilise them for food are known as **consumers** or **heterotrophs**. Primary consumers are herbivores while the animals that prey upon them are secondary consumers. They, in turn, form the food of larger carnivores or tertiary consumers. Each category of feeding is known as a **trophic level** from the Greek *trophos* which means a 'feeder'.

Some heterotrophs obtain their energy from dead and decaying material and are called **decomposers**. If they absorb soluble organic nutrients and are plants or plant-like, they are said to be **saprophytic**; if animals or animal-like, they are **saprozoitic**. The majority of decomposers are bacteria and fungi but others are Protista, some of which inhabit the alimentary canals of animals thus enabling them to break down cellulose and other plant compounds that cannot be digested by most animal enzymes. In addition to predators, some consumers are parasites, both of producers and of other consumers. Members of all five kingdoms (Appendix I) may adopt a parasitic mode of life. Such relationships form the basis of food chains and food webs (to be discussed below).

The carbon cycle

The logical place at which to begin the study of food chains is with chemosynthesis by plant. Because plants use so much of the energy obtained by photosynthesis in biochemical transformations, they always contain in their tissues much less energy than the total that they have assimilated. Ecologists therefore distinguish between gross primary production – the total energy assimilated – and net primary production – the energy stored in plant biomass. The difference between these two represents the energy used for biosynthesis, respiration and maintenance.

Primary production involves fluxes of carbon dioxide, oxygen, nitrogen, minerals and water. Gross production can be assessed by measuring growth rates, gas exchange and so on; net production as grams of carbon assimilated or the dry weight of plant tissues. The carbon cycle is closely associated with energy flow in the ecosystem (Figure 2.2). Indeed, next to water, carbon is the most significant component of living organisms and constitutes about 49 per cent of their dry weight.

Three major processes are involved in the cycling of carbon in both aquatic and terrestrial ecosystems. The first consists of the assimilation of carbon dioxide in photosynthesis and its loss in respiration. The second involves the physical exchange of carbon dioxide between the atmosphere, the oceans, lakes and rivers. Carbon dioxide is very soluble in water and there is about 50 times as much of this gas dissolved in the oceans of the world as there is in the atmosphere. The balance between consumption and production is, however, about the same on land as in water. Consequently, the carbon cycles of aquatic and terrestrial systems are virtually independent. It is not

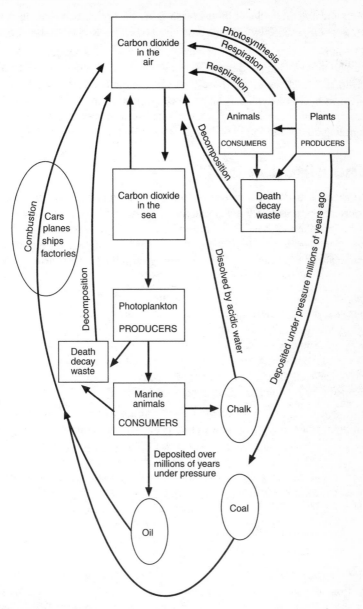

2.2 The carbon cycle.

yet known to what extent the increasing amounts of carbon dioxide in the atmosphere, caused by human activities, are being absorbed by the oceans.

The third major process in the cycling of carbon involves the solution of carbon dioxide and the deposition of carbonate compounds in the form of sediments such as chalk, limestone and dolomite. Removal of carbon dioxide by photosynthesis in the oceans results in the formation and precipitation of calcium carbonate – unless it is incorporated by reef-building corals and in the bodies of planktonic Foraminiferida (Protista).

The nitrogen cycle

Nitrogen is an essential element of amino acids and proteins. The ultimate source of nitrogen in the ecosystems of the world is gaseous nitrogen in the atmosphere. Although to some extent soluble in water, nitrogen does not combine with rock. Were it not for the biological fixation of atmospheric nitrogen, nearly all the nitrogen on the Earth's surface would still be in the form of atmospheric molecules.

Some plants (Leguminosae) have nodules on their roots which contain nitrogen-fixing bacteria (*Rhizobium*). These convert gaseous nitrogen into nitrogenous compounds from which plants can synthesise amino acids and proteins. Some free-living soil bacteria (*Azotobacter*) and cyanobacteria do the same. Before artificial fertilisers came into general use, crops were rotated annually and a crop of legumes – peas, beans or clover – was always planted every second or third year to enrich the soil.

Nitrogen combines with oxygen in the atmosphere to form oxides of nitrogen when electric current in the form of lightning passes through the gases. Gaseous oxides of nitrogen react with water to form nitric acid, which is washed into the ground by rain. Here it reacts with minerals to form nitrates. These are absorbed by plants through their roots and are later synthesised into proteins (Figure 2.3). The chemical reactions involved in the first stages of the nitrogen cycle are as follows:

$N_2 + 2 O_2 \rightarrow 2 NO_2$ (nitrous oxide)

$NO_2 + H_2O \rightarrow H_2 NO_3$ (nitric acid)

Herbivorous animals obtain protein by eating plants, the producers at the bottom of the food chain. Carnivores eat the flesh of other animals – **primary consumers** – which, in turn, have obtained protein from plants. Many animals are omnivores, feeding on both plant and animal material.

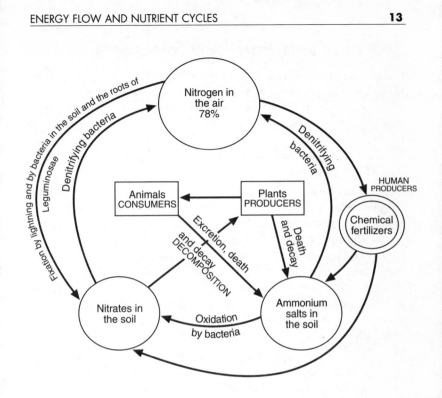

2.3 The nitrogen cycle.

The excreta and the products of decay of both plants and animals are broken down into ammonium salts which, in turn, are converted into nitrates by nitrifying bacteria. Nitrification, which involves the oxidation of nitrogen from ammonia to nitrites and then to nitrates, is also undertaken by specialised bacteria. The first stage is carried out by *Nitrosomonas* in the soil and by *Nitrosococcus* in the sea, the second by *Nitrobacter* in the soil and *Nitrococcus* in the oceans. Nitrification can only take place in the presence of oxygen. Under **anoxic** conditions, as in waterlogged soils where there is no oxygen, the reactions are reversed and unpleasant smells result. Both nitrates and ammonium salts are removed from the soil by denitrifying bacteria, which convert them back to nitrogen which is returned to the atmosphere. Thus the loop of the nitrogen cycle is completed (Figure 2.3).

Soil nutrients and trace elements

Carbon and nitrogen are not the only elements to be cycled through the biosphere. The **phosphorus cycle** has been studied intensively because living organisms require about one-tenth as much phosphorus as they do nitrogen. It is a constituent of nucleic acids, cell membranes, bones, teeth and so on. The phosphorus cycle is simpler than the nitrogen cycle because plants can assimilate phosphorus directly from soil or water in the form of phosphate ($-PO_4$).

Phosphorus does not enter the atmosphere except as dust and the phosphorus cycle involves only soil and water. Animals excrete excess organic phosphorus in their urine so that it becomes available again to plants. The phosphorus cycle is closely related to the acidity of the soil. In acid conditions it binds tightly to clay particles forming insoluble compounds with ferric iron. Under alkaline conditions, on the other hand, it forms insoluble compounds with calcium. The concentration of dissolved phosphate in equilibrium with insoluble compounds therefore depends upon the acidity of the soil and the presence of iron, calcium and aluminium.

Many other elements are required for the metabolism of plants and animals. **Major elements** required in the diet of humans, for instance, include calcium, sodium, chlorine, phosphorus, sulphur, potassium and magnesium, as well as smaller quantities of the **trace elements** iron, fluorine, iodine, zinc, copper and cobalt. Specific deficiency diseases occur when any of these essential minerals is lacking.

Many of the chemical reactions and cycles discussed above are accomplished mainly or even entirely by microorganisms. Without their intervention, the productivity of the ecosystem would be much reduced. The energy transformations for which they are responsible take place mainly during oxidation-reduction (**redox**) reactions. The elements in organic compounds tend to be in reduced form. Consequently their assimilation requires energy. Those in an oxidised form gain energy when they are reduced, while those that are reduced release energy upon being oxidised.

Interaction between productivity and consumption

Biotic interactions are involved in numerous ways in addition to the basic interactions between living organisms involved in the gaseous carbon and nitrogen cycles. They take part in the **sedimentary nutrient** cycles of sulphur, phosphorus and various trace elements. In these the gaseous phase (e.g. sulphur dioxide) is relatively insignificant.

Primary production involves fluxes of carbon dioxide, oxygen, nitrogen and other elements, as well as of minerals on one hand and the accumulation of plant biomass on the other. Net production may be expressed as grams of carbon assimilated, the dry weight of plant tissues, or the equivalents of these in joules (J), which are the SI units of energy (4.182 J = 1 calorie). In terrestrial ecosystems, plant production is usually estimated by measurements of the annual increase in biomass. In most habitats this is limited by nutrient deficiency. That is why the application of fertilisers containing compounds of nitrogen, phosphorus, or both usually stimulates the growth of plants.

Limitation of nutrients is especially marked in aquatic environments where production depends upon the rapid assimilation of regenerated nutrients within the **photic** or sunlit zone. Most of these differ from terrestrial habitats in that their nutrients tend to accumulate in deposits on the bottom from which they are regenerated only slowly and returned to the zones of production. The sediments in aquatic systems can be compared with the detritus layer in terrestrial habitats, but the latter differs from them in two ways. First, the regeneration of nutrients from terrestrial detritus takes place near the roots of the plants and, secondly, decomposition is mainly aerobic on land and therefore takes place comparatively rapidly. In aquatic habitats, as in waterlogged soil, sediments and detritus often become anoxic and most biochemical reactions are therefore considerably slowed down.

The law of limiting factors

In 1840, the German chemist Justus von Liebig published a treatise on *Chemistry in its Application to Agriculture and Physiology*. In this he noted that: 'The crops of a field diminish or increase in exact proportion to the diminution or increase of the mineral substances conveyed to it in nature.'

As originally conceptualised, Liebig's **Law of the minimum** applied only to inorganic nutrients but it was later expanded to include physical factors such as temperature and rainfall. F.F. Blackman extended it even further in 1905 to encompass the limiting effects of the maximum as well. In what has become known as the **Law of limiting factors** Blackman distinguished three cardinal points: 'the *minimal* condition below which the phenomenon ceases altogether, the *optimal* condition at which it is exhibited to its highest observed degree, and the *maximal* condition above which it ceases again.'

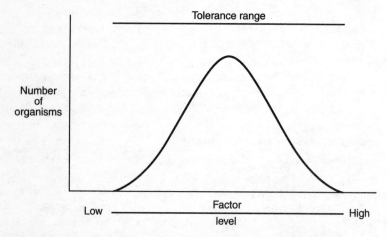

2.4 Principle of the law of toleration (after E.J. Kormandy).

Victor E. Shelford incorporated both the geographical environment and the ecological physiology of organisms in his **Law of toleration**. In 1911 he stated that 'the *law of the minimum* is but a special case of the *law of toleration*. Combinations of the factors which fall under the law of the minimum may be made, which make the law of toleration apply quite generally' (Figure 2.4). Living organisms have differing ranges of tolerance to different environmental factors and function best in the central points of these ranges. Those species with wide ranges of tolerance to a variety of environmental factors are likely to be the most widely distributed. The law of limiting factors has been formulated principally with respect to the plant kingdom, but can be extended to incorporate animals and other living organisms as well.

Resource limitation in food chains

The level of any resource is limited by consumption and, by limiting their resources, consumers may limit the sizes of their own populations. Whereas resources are inevitably reduced by consumption, by no means all resources limit the populations of their consumers. For instance, although animals require oxygen for respiration, they do not depress the level of this gas in the atmosphere because some other resource, such as food supply, water, nutrients or available shelter, limits population growth long before atmospheric oxygen becomes depleted. The potential of any resources to limit population growth depends upon the ratio of its availability to demand. Some resources, such as food and light, are renewable whereas others (e.g. space) are not. This is a major problem facing the ever-increasing population of human beings. When one non-renewable resource has been depleted, something else must always be found to take its place. Food webs are networks of consumer–resource interactions among groups of organisms, populations or aggregate trophic units. Three basic approaches can be used in their investigation:

1 Static description of feeding links (either observed or estimated) among species or **guilds**. These are assemblages of species that use the environment in the same way;

2 Quantification of the transport of energy via predation within guilds;

3 Identification of those feeding links that are most influential in the dynamics of community composition and structure.

Food chains, food webs and ecological pyramids

Food chains are seldom simple. They illustrate the passage of food and, therefore, of energy from producers to the organisms that feed upon them. These primary consumers are the food of secondary consumers and so on. The number of links in a food chain between producer and top predator may vary, but seldom exceeds five. For example, grass → sheep → humans, or algae (producers) → crustaceans (primary consumers) → fishes (secondary consumers) → seals (tertiary consumers) → killer whales (top carnivores). There may be intermediate links in a food chain, for example when small crustaceans are eaten by larger crustaceans, smaller fishes by

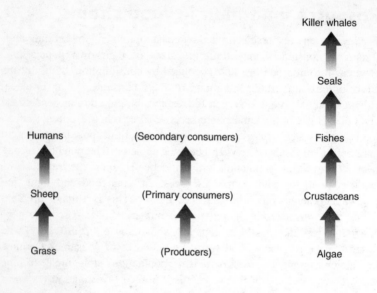

2.5 Food chains in the sea and on land.

larger ones. Food chains can also be shortened, for instance when crustaceans (krill: *Ephausia superba*) are eaten by baleen whales (Figure 2.5) (*see* Chapter 5).

Most communities contain several food chains which link with one another to form **food webs**. This is because the diets of most animals consist of a number of different items. Furthermore, secondary consumers often feed on the primary consumers of more than one food chain, while omnivores are both producers or consumers depending whether they are feeding on plants or on other animals (Figure 2.6).

Food webs indicate the feeding relationships that occur in communities, but give no indication about the numbers of individuals involved. It takes many plants to support fewer herbivores and these herbivores support even fewer carnivores. Thousands of leaves are required to feed hundreds of caterpillars. These, in turn, provide the food for tens of warblers which themselves may support only a single hawk. At each link in a food chain the amount of biomass is reduced to at least one-tenth of that present in

the previous link. Consequently every ecosystem can be represented as a
pyramid of numbers (Figure 2.7 a,b).

Pyramids of numbers are not without shortcomings. If parasites are
included, they distort and may even invert the pyramid because one host
can support very large numbers of parasites. Not only do the numbers of
organisms decrease with each ascending link of a food chain, but their sizes
increase correspondingly. Hawks are larger than warblers which, in turn, are
much larger than caterpillars. The problem can, to some extent, be
overcome by constructing a pyramid of biomass. A representative sample of
the organisms at each trophic level is oven-dried at 110 °C until it no longer

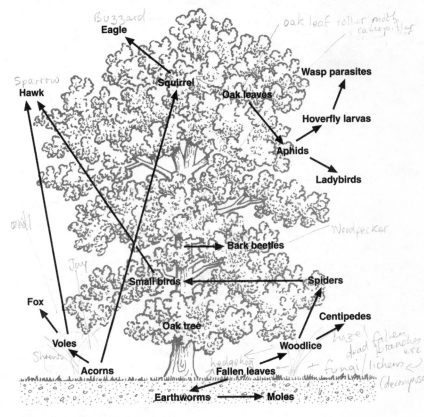

**2.6 A simplified temperate forest food web based on
an oak tree.**

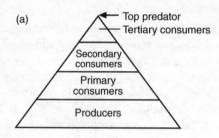

(a) Top predator
Tertiary consumers
Secondary consumers
Primary consumers
Producers

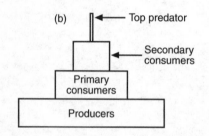

(b) Top predator
Secondary consumers
Primary consumers
Producers

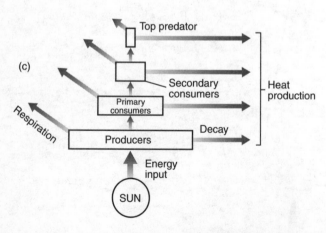

(c) Top predator
Secondary consumers
Primary consumers
Respiration
Producers
Decay
Heat production
Energy input
SUN

2.7 Ecological pyramids. (a) Pyramid of numbers; (b) Pyramid of biomass; (c) Pyramid of energy flow.

loses any weight. Its mass is then multiplied to bring it up to the estimated number of organisms at that trophic level dry mass is normally used because fresh mass varies so much depending upon its water content (Figure 2.6c).

Biomass pyramids also have their drawbacks. Some organisms, such as grasses, may grow very rapidly but their biomass is relatively small. Others, such as deciduous trees, may have greater mass when in full leaf in the summer than they have in winter when the leaves have fallen. Again, the biomass of most animals is usually greater just after the breeding season than it is at other times of the year. **Pyramids of energy** provide the most accurate representation of energy flow and the feeding relationships of the organisms in an ecosystem. They can be used to compare land use in different communities, or the productivity of different methods of farming. But, at best, they can only provide approximations of what is taking place in the infinitely complex situations of the natural world.

The regulation of ecosystems

Three methods are used to study the regulation of ecosystems: comparison, experiment and modelling. The results of experiments are best interpreted when compared with the predictions of mathematical models based on the known mechanisms by which ecosystems function. Study of ecosystems shows that primary production, controlled by limiting factors, in turn limits the resources upon which food chains are based. In his book *The Elements of Physical Biology*, A.J. Lotka (1925) was the first to apply **systems models** to ecological systems. He showed that the flux of an element that was being cycled is not sensitive to variation in the smallest transfer rate. The mathematics involved in his work is complicated, but he was able to outline the application of systems modelling to the interpretation of nutrient cycling in ecosystems. For instance, when a system is in a steady state, relative transfer rates can be estimated from compartment size. Thus, for a sample model of nitrogen cycling within the water column of a lake, seasonal changes in nitrogen compartments indicate that the assimilation of nitrates decreases dramatically in winter. The reader who can understand mathematical work of this kind will, however, have graduated well beyond the scope of *Teach Yourself Ecology*!

3 | ANALYSIS OF THE ENVIRONMENT

The biosphere in which living organisms are found has two components – the living and the non-living. Even the most staunch supporters of the Gaia hypothesis will agree that these two great realms of the natural world, the animate and the inanimate, are almost always distinguishable and separate, although they are by no means independent of one another – which, of course, is the main thesis of Gaia. Life depends upon the physical world. At the same time, the physical world is greatly influenced by living organisms. Without photosynthesis the atmosphere would be devoid of oxygen. So would the soil, lakes and oceans. Indeed, as we shall soon see, plants and animals have a striking influence on soil formation. The major, non-living, components of the environment are climate and geology.

Climate

Climate may be interpreted in terms of the movement of air masses and the way these interact when they converge. A **front** occurs where two distinct air masses with different characteristics come into contact with one another. In temperate regions, fronts are usually marked by differences in temperature between the adjacent air masses. In the tropics there is usually no such contrast in temperature, the only differences being in their humidity and stability.

Solar radiation is the source of atmospheric energy, and its distribution over the world not only controls the climate but is, itself, a climatic element of the greatest ecological importance. The amount received at any latitude depends both upon the angle at which the sunlight strikes the curved atmosphere of the Earth and on the duration of day length at that season of the year.

If the Earth were not rotating, its atmosphere would circulate in the form of two gigantic **convectional** systems. (Convection in this context means the transfer of heat from warmer to cooler parts of the atmosphere by the flow of air.) Air warmed in equatorial regions rises, flows towards the poles at high levels and there gives up its heat. At the same time, cold polar air flows back towards the equator nearer to the surface of the Earth. The atmospheric pressure at intermediate or **horse latitudes** is high. Because the Earth is rotating, however, the **trade winds** which blow from the horse latitudes towards the **equatorial trough** or **doldrums** come from the north-east and south-east instead of from the north and south respectively. The direction of the other planetary wind systems is also affected not only by the Earth's rotation but also by the irregular shapes and distribution of the continents and oceans.

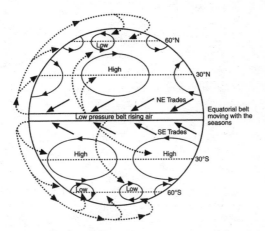

3.1 Planetary wind systems.

The equatorial trough is centred near to latitude 5°N in January and around 12–15°N in July. It migrates through some 20° latitude between seasons. This migration brings seasonal rainfall and is responsible for the formation of tropical storms. Since the annual mean equatorial trough lies near 5°N rather than on the geographical equator, this latitude is often known as the **meteorological equator**. (A classification of world climates and their vegetation is given in Appendix II.)

Not only do living organisms receive their energy from sunlight, but they tolerate extremes of radiation, temperature, moisture, salinity and so on.

Ultra-violet (UV) **radiation** is extremely harmful to life. It is divided into three components: UVA which darkens the human skin and causes a tan to develop. This does not burn, but may damage deeper levels of the skin. UVB burns the skin and, in excess, is a major cause of **melanoma** (cancer arising from the pigment-producing cells). It is particularly harmful to worms, amphibians and other animals with delicate, unprotected skins. UVC radiation (below 200 nm) is also very harmful to skin, but is mostly filtered out by the ozone layer of the upper atmosphere. That is why so much concern is currently being expressed at the reduction of the ozone layer through the action of artificial **chlorofluorocarbons** (CFCs) used as refrigerants and to pressurise spray cans.

Greenhouse gases

Levels of carbon dioxide in the atmosphere appear to have increased in recent years as a result of industrial pollution of the atmosphere through excessive burning of fossil fuels and destruction of the world's forests for commercial interests, thereby producing the so-called 'greenhouse' effect. Long-wave (heat) radiation from the Earth's surface is now absorbed and retained to a greater extent than previously by the atmosphere. In consequence, the temperature of the Earth may be steadily increasing. It is expected to rise by 2–6 °C during the next century – with untold consequences for human beings. If the polar ice caps melt, the level of the oceans will rise and low-lying ports and cities will be submerged. Agriculture may be disrupted and ecosystems shifted across the landscape.

Methane (CH_4) is another greenhouse gas whose concentration in the atmosphere has been rising at an enormous rate – roughly one to two per cent per year. No one yet knows exactly why. It may be the result of increased cultivation of rice which grows in stagnant waterlogged fields, or perhaps because the large populations of cattle maintained in the world today produce so much dung. The combined effects of modern technology and the human population explosion present a serious threat to the future of humanity (this subject will be discussed further in Chapter 11). We shall now consider the individual components of climate.

High temperature

Global patterns in temperature and rainfall are engendered by variations in solar radiation at different latitudes. The climate of the world tends to be hot and wet near the equator, cold and dry towards the poles. We shall consider the effects of this in Chapter 4. We are concerned here with the direct effects of temperature on living organisms. The processes of life on Earth can only take place between the freezing and boiling points of water, although some living organisms are able, temporarily, to withstand even greater extremes.

That any animal could tolerate a temperature of 104 °C for more than an hour, or withstand immersion in liquid helium (–270 °C), may stretch credulity to its limits but nonetheless it is true. *Polypedilum vanderplancki* (Figure 3.2a) is a midge in West Africa whose larvae inhabit the small pools that form in shallow hollows on unshaded rocks during the rainy season. These hollows may fill up and dry out several times each year, but the larvae are well adapted to their unstable environment. They can absorb water and then become almost completely desiccated many times without suffering harm. They may persist in a dehydrated state for decades and are then able to survive exposure to extremely high and low temperatures. In the active, hydrated state, however, their thermal tolerances are no different from those of any other midge larvae. Howard Hinton of Bristol University, who investigated these insects shortly after the Second World War, found that you can even cut a dehydrated larva in two and keep it for years. When you place the halves in water, however, they absorb moisture and begin to wriggle. Then, because they have already been cut in half, they die!

Some insects and other animals endure unfavourable climatic conditions in a metabolically inactive state known as **diapause**. (In the same way, the seeds of annual plants may survive cold winters or hot, dry summers in diapause.) Any stage of an insect's life cycle can enter diapause, but the egg is the one that most frequently does so. Whilst in diapause, the eggs are resistant to heat, cold and drought. Tadpole shrimps (*Triops* spp.) (Figure 3.2b) and other inhabitants of ephemeral desert rain pools survive the hot, dry summer in the form of diapause eggs. These eggs may tolerate 98 °C for 16 hours whilst dry, but the lethal temperature of the active adults, which are not in diapause, is only 40 °C for 2 hours or 34 °C for 24 hours.

Some desert animals are able to withstand unusually high temperatures without any special ecophysiological adaptations. These include the Sudanese camel-spider *Galeodes granti* (Solifugae) (Figure 3.3) which can tolerate exposure to 50 °C for up to 24 hours at relative humidities below 10 per cent, and the scorpion *Leiurus quinquestriatus* which tolerates 47 °C for the same length of time (Figure 3.4).

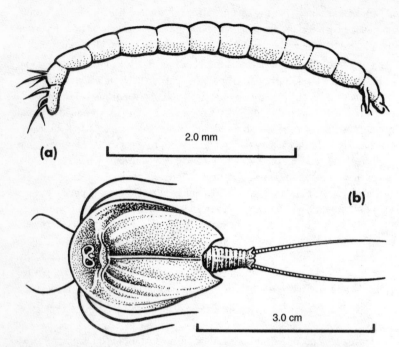

3.2 **(a)** *Polypedilum vanderplancki* larva; **(b)** *Triops granarius*: two species that survive thermal extremes using different physiologcal mechanisms.

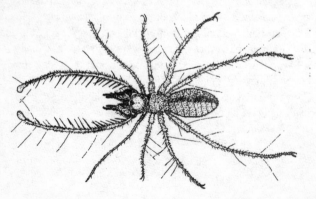

3.3 *Galeodes granti* (body length 8cm).

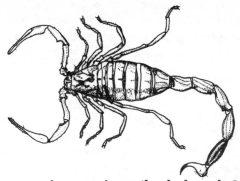

3.4 *Leiurus quinquestriatus* **(body length 8cm).**

Cold

When plants and animals freeze, the ice that is formed within their cells may cause so much damage to the cell membranes that the cells are killed. Many species that inhabit regions in which the winters are cold survive either by resisting freezing or by tolerating its effects. The hardening of plants so that they can withstand freezing takes place in stages as temperatures drop during autumn. Persistent frost leads to complete **frost hardiness** and some Arctic species are even able to survive temporary immersion in liquid nitrogen at –196 °C.

Animals may be adapted in several ways to life in cold environments. Birds and mammals of polar regions are well insulated by thick fur, feathers or, in the case of seals and whales, a layer of fat or blubber beneath the skin. In addition, their bodies are stout with short limbs and ears, thereby reducing their surface areas.

Animal cells are less likely to be damaged if freezing takes place rapidly so that they become solidified with amorphous non-crystalline ice. Thawing has to be equally rapid so that ice crystals do not form and puncture the cell membranes during the melting process. Many organisms are able to reduce the freezing points of their body fluids by secreting up to 30 per cent of glycerol and glycoproteins, which act like the anti-freeze in a car radiator. **Supercooling** to –8 °C has been recorded in fishes and reptiles and down to –18 °C among some invertebrates.

Different regional floras and faunas vary in their tolerance of frost. Many tropical and subtropical organisms are unable to withstand cooler temperatures, even though these may be way above freezing. An enormous variety of thermal barriers limits the distribution of plants and animals. Where these limitations are due to variations in metabolic rates, their effects can be extremely subtle.

Rainfall and humidity

The availability of moisture exerts an enormous effect on the distribution of plants and, to a lesser extent, of animals. In general, animals are able to move about in search of water, whereas plants can grow only where it is available. At the same time, since animal life relies ultimately upon plants for food, animals are dependent upon the vegetation for their existence. In Chapter 4 we shall see how the terrestrial biomes of the world are determined by the combination of precipitation and temperature.

Tropical regions where the rainfall is high are exceptionally rich in the numbers of individuals and species present. Plant growth is rapid although essential soil nutrients may be scarce. In arid regions, on the other hand, the annual growth period of both flora and fauna is much reduced. The hot, dry season may be passed, as we have seen, in diapause. In the case of perennial plants, every facet of adaptation, from the morphology of leaves, stems and roots to the timing of germination, growth and flowering, is adjusted so that survival is possible with the supply of moisture that is available. Likewise, desert animals are adapted for life in arid conditions.

Oxygen

The absence of oxygen may present a problem for higher animals and it is not certain whether life in the complete absence of oxygen is possible for them – although many species can exist without oxygen for long periods of time. A small crustacean (*Thermocyclops schuurmanni*), however, has been found to exist for at least part of its life in the oxygen-free depths of African volcanic lakes, while other crustaceans inhabit brine and soda lakes.

Geology

Geology is the study of the rocks of the Earth's crust. Some rocks are hard and can only be broken by a sharp blow with a hammer. Others, such as sandstones, are relatively soft and can even be excavated by sand martins and other birds. Limestones, such as chalk, are **alkaline** or **basic**, while quartzites are **acid**. The physical and chemical properties of the underlying rock affect the soil that is formed from them and hence the distribution of plants and animals.

The oldest rocks originated from the molten **magma** of the interior of the Earth. When this cools and becomes solid, it forms **igneous crystalline** rock such as granite and diorite. If molten rock cools slowly, large crystals are formed – as in the basalts of the Giant's Causeway on the northern coast of Ireland. When it cools quickly, however, like the lava flows from a volcano, the crystals are very small. **Obsidian** or volcanic glass has cooled extremely rapidly and contains no crystals at all.

During the ages, some crystalline rocks have been subjected to weathering. The crystals have been broken down by the action of water, sun, frost, chemical and biological agents. The resulting mineral particles, transported by rivers, and occasionally by wind, usually find their way into the sea. Here they settle on the bottom, forming deposits which may become extremely thick. Eventually these deposits become consolidated to form **sedimentary** rocks. The material that forms sedimentary rocks may have been transported from land to sea many times during the history of the Earth. Other sedimentary rocks are of organic origin and include chalk and coal. Sedimentary rocks are softer and more easily weathered than igneous rocks. They are also more permeable to water.

Metamorphic rocks, such as quartzite and marble, are formed by heat and pressure on sandstone and calcareous sedimentary rocks. They are rather unimportant biologically: igneous and sedimentary rocks are the principal sources of the mineral fraction of the soil. Some rocks, including igneus rocks, may undergo more than one episode of metamorphic recrystallisation.

Soils

Soils develop through weathering of the parent rocks that make up the crust of the Earth. In addition to this mineral substrate, in which vegetation takes root, soils include dead organic matter and humus, water and air. Weathering of the rocks to produce the **parent material** of the soil is usually achieved by a combination of three processes:

1 **Mechanical weathering**, in which breakdown of the rock itself occurs without chemical change;

2 **Chemical weathering**, where an actual chemical change of the rock minerals takes place and new substances are formed;

    3 Biological weathering, where the agents of change are living organisms which employ mechanical and chemical processes.

Plants and animals, dead and alive, play an important role in weathering. Their actions facilitate the entrance of air and water, thereby contributing to the physical and chemical processes involved. Plant roots disintegrate rocks by the pressure they exert in crevices thereby assisting mechanical weathering, while their tips secrete acid which dissolves the alkaline minerals with which it comes into contact. Decaying plant and animal remains produce carbon dioxide. Since bacteria and fungi are largely responsible for this decay they too must be regarded as being contributory to the other agents of chemical weathering.

Soil consists of a mixture of mineral particles, humus, air and water. The mineral fraction consists mainly of silica or quartz and potassium aluminium silicate often combined with iron, magnesium and small quantities of other substances. Calcium carbonate in the form of chalk and limestone often imparts characteristic properties to the soil overlying it.

Soil profiles

As the result of weathering, a characteristic layered arrangement known as a **soil profile** is developed. This depends largely upon the amount and kind of organic matter present and also upon the way in which water falling on the surface removes and redeposits the soluble constituents of the surface layers. Under humid conditions, soluble salts are **leached** away but, where water is scarce, **pedocals**, or soils rich in calcium, are formed. **Pedalfers**, or leached soils, occur under humid conditions where rainfall is in excess of potential evaporation.

A typical soil profile consists of several **horizons** (Figure 3.5) each having characteristic physical and chemical properties. At the surface there is frequently a layer of undecomposed material, the litter or L layer (often called Fö layer, from the Swedish term, *Förna*). Beneath this lies the humus or A_0 layer, composed of amorphous organic matter which has lost its original structure. Then comes a varying number of A layers of true soil. The first of these, A_1, is a dark-coloured horizon containing a relatively high content of organic matter mixed with mineral fragments. It tends to be thick in savanna and thin in forest soils. The A_2 horizon is frequently ashy grey and is the zone of maximum leaching. The underlying B horizons tend to be darker in colour because they are

L or Fo	Litter layer
A_0	Humus layer
A_1	Dark horizon with high organic content
A_2	Light-coloured leached horizon
A_3 and B_1	Transitional
B_2	Dark zone of maximum receipt of transported colloids
B_3	Transitional (sometimes G)
C	Parent material
D	Underlying rock

3.5 Nomenclature of soil horizons.

enriched by iron compounds, clay and humus. A lighter coloured C horizon of parent material then grades into the D horizon of bed rock.

This description is applicable to **podsols** (Figure 3.6), acid soils with strongly acid hydrogen ion concentration (usually below pH 5.5) and excessive drainage. Podsols are developed on sandstones under conditions of moderately heavy rainfall. In **brown earths** or **brown forest earths**, the profile is less uniformly coloured throughout, with a darker humus-rich A_1 horizon on top which grades into slightly lighter coloured subsoil. Brown earths are usually slightly acid and certainly never alkaline. They are frequently developed over clays and drainage is often slow.

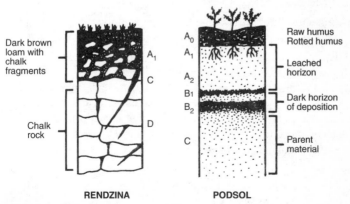

RENDZINA   PODSOL

3.6 Rendzina, which develops over chalk, and podsol profiles.

Although the soils in equatorial and tropical rainforest do not become very acid, high temperatures throughout the year cause clay materials to decompose quite rapidly and the silica fraction especially becomes very mobile. It is leached downwards and either deposited in the weathering material below or else removed altogether with drainage water. The upper horizons become relatively rich in compounds of iron and aluminium and are predominantly red in colour. They are referred to as **laterite** or tropical red soils. In Tsavo National Park in Kenya the elephants really are pink when covered with laterite dust!

Although laterisation is widespread in the tropics, it does not occur everywhere. Where the parent material is composed of porous sandstone, quartzite or grit and the clay content small, percolation is rapid. A deep A_0 horizon of acid peat with a typical podsol beneath, then develops. Brown earth soil is found under tropical steppe and savanna grassland but in many places it is neither black nor calcareous as it is in temperate steppes. In more arid regions the soil types usually formed are brown or grey semi-desert soils. They contain little organic matter and calcium carbonate is frequently deposited on the soil surface. Desert soils are produced almost entirely by physical weathering. They contain no humus and are little more than fragmented rock.

The soil profile reflects the features of surface relief as well as the parental rock. Shallow soils develop in hilly regions where run-off and erosion are excessive. Flat land experiences little erosion and a leached upper soil develops over a dense clay pan: low-lying regions with poor drainage tend to accumulate humus.

The elements of the environment whose combinations determine the nature of soils are known as **edaphic factors** (from the Greek *edaphos* meaning floor or earth). As every gardener knows, some plants thrive on alkaline soils, others require acid humus in which to grow. Some need moisture and shade, others must have well drained soil with a sunny aspect. Animals, too, are influenced by edaphic factors. Woodlice and snails are far more numerous on alkaline than on acid soil. They require calcium carbonate for their integuments and shells respectively. Salinity is another important edaphic factor.

Habitat and niche

Every living organism typically inhabits a particular locality or **habitat**. At any given latitude, some habitats support more species and/or individuals than others do, depending on their productivity, structural complexity and the suitability of their physical conditions. For example, grassland might be home to 6 species of birds, shrubland to 14, coniferous forest to 17 and deciduous forest to 21. Species diversity is greater in more complex habitats whereas mere numbers and biomass are only dependent upon productivity.

To give an example of habitats, the pond community of the deciduous forest biome can be divided into the following:

1 The **water's edge** with reed mace and other plants growing beside it;

2 The **surface** of the pond occupied by microscopic plants and animals, duckweed, pond skaters, whirligig beetles and so on;

3 **Clear water** containing planktonic Protista, crustaceans, water beetles and fishes;

4 The **bottom** with water lilies and other aquatic plants rooted in it, dragon-fly larvae crawling about, tadpoles feeding on algae and the various invertebrates associated with them;

5 **Detritus**.

When pond organisms die, they sink to the bottom and form a muddy layer along with leaves, rotting twigs and other matter that falls into the pond from outside. The layer of detritus is inhabited by bacteria, fungi, nematodes, blood worms (*Tubifex*) and others. The top predator of the food chain might well be a heron which devours the fish that feed on the tadpoles which eat the algae (Figure 3.7). Many inhabitants of the pond community move from one of these habitats to another. Beetles and tadpoles swim to the bottom to feed on detritus; water lilies have their roots growing at the bottom while their leaves are floating on the surface. Some animals occupy two or more quite different habitats such as heaths and fens which, to the human observer, appear to have very little in common. This can be very confusing and may require complex explanation (*see* Chapter 7).

In general, more species occur in the tropics than in temperate regions, whilst comparatively few are found in the Arctic and Antarctic. This is because more ecological **niches** are exploited in the tropics. Every species

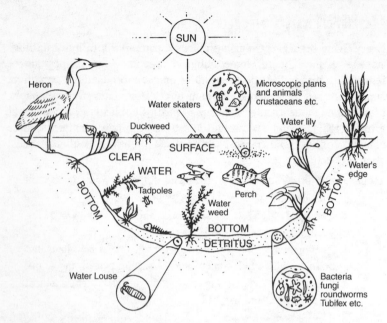

3.7   Habitats in a temperate pond community (modified after D.G. Applin).

occupies a niche determined, in the case of animals, by the nature of its food and consequently of its size. Thus, among the carnivores of a temperate woodland community there may be predator niches occupied by foxes, badgers, stoats, weasels and shrews among mammals, while hawks and owls are diurnal and nocturnal avian predators respectively. The niche or activity range of each species embraces every dimension of the environment including physical, chemical and biological factors, time of day and season of year.

Cursorial adaptations

The terrestrial habitat is home to animals that are adapted to life on land. Those that live in open country often have **cursorial** adaptations which enable them to run fast. Speed is achieved by increasing the length of the limb, especially the distal bones furthest from the body. For example, the limbs of horses are elongated distally by the formation of cannon bones from the metatarsals of the third digit. All the other toes have been lost during the course of evolution and the humerus and femur are comparatively short. This lightens the limb so that it can be moved rapidly and the length of the stride increased. The principle invoked is that of the pendulum. The shorter it is, the faster its rate of swing (Figure 3.8). In order to speed a pendulum clock, the weight or 'bob' must be raised. Now, if the weight represents the main locomotory muscles and their insertions, a long, fast moving limb can be achieved by shortening the proximal bones, that is the ones nearer to the body, and elongating the distal ones.

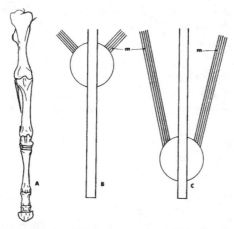

3.8   Pendulum principle of mammalian limbs. (a) Hind limb of horse, showing pulley-like joints for restriction of movement to one plane; (b) Pendulum with 'bob' raised for rapid swing; (c) Pendulum with 'bob' lowered giving slow swing but greater leverage from the muscles (m).

Burrowing adaptations

In contrast, burrowing animals such as mole crickets, moles and mole rats tend to have very short and powerful limbs. Shortening is particularly marked in the distal bones so that the angle of insertion of the muscles is less than it is in cursorial species and greater leverage obtained (Figure 3.8).

Scansorial adaptations

Many forest animals adopt an arboreal life. They often have **scansorial** adaptations for climbing, although some, such as leopards, jaguars, pangolins and rodents, can climb quite well without possessing any marked adaptations. The majority of tree-dwellers are **branch runners**. They live and move on all fours on the upper surfaces of the branches. Sloths, in contrast, hang suspended beneath the branches by their powerful curved claws. Some monkeys and apes are **brachiators** and swing from branch to branch by their fore limbs. African and Asian monkeys do not have **prehensile** tails which can be used for grasping, as do some of their New World relatives, but they are usually much better climbers. Chameleons and arboreal snakes also have prehensile tails but tend to move slowly.

The feet of arboreal animals may be prehensile or non-prehensile. In the latter, the claws are usually well developed – as in squirrels and cats. Prehensile hands and feet are modified for grasping by one or more of the digits being opposed to the others. Opposable digits are found in parrots and other birds, chameleons and opossums. Primates have an opposable thumb and, except in humans, an opposable big toe as well. Adhesive pads are sometimes found, either on the tips of the digits, as in treefrogs and geckoes, or on the soles of the feet of arboreal animals.

Aerial adaptations

Several kinds of animals have developed the ability to fly. Only insects, birds and bats are capable of sustained flight, as were the extinct pterodactyls, but many others can glide for considerable distances. These include flying fishes, flying frogs, flying lizards of various kinds, flying snakes, flying phalangers, flying squirrels, flying lemurs and so on (Figure 3.9).

Insects are the only animals whose wings have not evolved from pre-existing limbs. It is believed that they represent development of the lobes of the thorax and that flying insects evolved from roach-like flightless ancestors in Carboniferous times. According to one hypothesis, these escaped from early spiders by jumping from the tree-ferns in which they lived and gliding to safety with the aid of large thoracic lobes which later evolved into wings. Another hypothesis suggests that flying insects may have evolved from smaller ancestors carried by wind into the upper air. Those with larger lobes were better able to glide in a controlled fashion and were therefore the most successful.

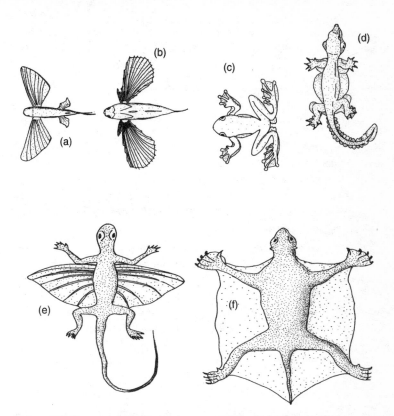

3.9   Gliding animals (not to scale): (a) Flying fish (*Exocoetus*); (b) Flying gurnard (*Dactylopterus*); (c) Flying frog (*Rhacophorus*); (d) Flying gecko (*Ptychozöon*); (e) Flying dragon (*Draco*); (f) Flying phalanger (*Galeopithecus*).

Flying fishes of various families use expanded fins as wings, while flying frogs glide with the help of the webbed digits of their large feet. In present-day flying reptiles, the body is flattened and extended sideways by a pair of wing-like membranes supported by elongated ribs. Flying phalangers and flying squirrels, on the other hand, glide on a fold of skin or **patagium** stretched between the limbs on either side of the body. The pterodactyls had a wing membrane supported by the little finger, which was enormously enlarged. The bird's wing consists of feathers attached to three digits of the forelimb which are more or less fused together while, in bats, all the digits are employed to some extent in supporting the wing membrane.

Aquatic adaptations

Most Protista are aquatic and swim by means of one or two thread-like **flagella**, or by **cilia** – the microscopic appendages that cover their cells. Cilia are normally 2 to 10 μm in length whereas flagella are very much longer, usually considerably exceeding the length of the cell that bears them. Many other aquatic animals creep on the surfaces of the ocean floor or river beds. Yet others are adapted for floating, with numerous hairs and spines which reduce the rate of sinking, gelatinous tissues and floats which lower their specific gravity.

The **plankton** of oceans and lakes consists of small organisms which tend to drift with the currents of the water. Plankton gets it name from the Greek *plagktos* which means 'wandering'. The **phytoplankton**, or 'plant' plankton, mostly composed of microsocpic single-celled diatoms and other plant-like Protista, carries out photosynthesis and forms the basis of aquatic food chains. The **zooplankton** – composed of animals which feed on the diatoms and other phytoplankton – usually has weak locomotory powers. It includes protozoans or animal-like Protista, small crustaceans and, in early summer, the larval stages of jelly-fish (Cnidaria), marine worms and other larger organisms.

Finally, at the top of the food chain are the predatory fishes, seals and whales with streamlined bodies adapted for rapid swimming. It is interesting that the very largest of all marine animals, basking sharks and baleen whales, are filter feeders and therefore low in the oceanic food chain. They need to eat so much that only small planktonic animals can reproduce quickly enough to satisfy their enormous appetites!

Evolutionary parallels

More homogeneous environments normally contain fewer species of plants and animals than do heterogenous, more diverse environments. Moreover, the most numerous species of animals tend to occupy the most extensive habitats – such as wide expanses of ocean or grassland. The extreme physical and climatic conditions of the desert biome have engendered or enhanced a number of structural, behavioural and physiological adaptations, many of which are paralleled by quite unrelated animals and even by plants. For instance, the leaves and stems of desert plants are frequently oriented so that the heat load from solar radiation is reduced.

There is a parallel here with the orientation of the 'compass' nests of termites in the Australian desert. These are oriented, with their narrow edges pointing in a north–south direction, as are the pads of cacti in Mexico and Arizona. This results in their sides being warmed at dawn and dusk when the temperature of the air is low while, at midday, a relatively small area faces the Sun. By cutting through such mounds at the base and rotating them through 90°, Gordon Grigg of the University of Sydney proved that the normal orientation prevents overheating. In winter, the termites aggregate on the East side of their mound in the morning and on the West in the afternoon. In summer, they retreat to the base or beneath ground level at midday.

Again, locusts orient their bodies at right angles to the Sun's rays in the morning and evening. At midday, however, when the heat is great, they turn their heads towards the Sun, thereby reducing the surface exposed to radiant heat. Ostriches, camels, wildebeest, springbok and many other species of antelope do the same. So do reptiles, while the leaves of plants by wilting reduce the area exposed to radiation.

Although completely unrelated, termites (Isoptera) and ants (Hymenoptera) have undergone parallel evolution and developed surprisingly similar social systems. As they are both insects, this is not altogether surprising, but who could possibly imagine that a species of mammal would have done the same thing? Yet the naked mole-rat (*Heterocephalus glaber*) of East Africa has done exactly that and has been studied since 1967 by Jennifer Jarvis of the University of Cape Town.

In the mid-1970s Richard D. Alexander, a professor at the University of Michigan, lectured on the evolution of social behaviour at several universities in the western United States and hypothesised a mythical mammal that would probably be a completely subterranean rodent which fed on large tubers and lived in burrows inaccessible to predators in a dry tropical region with heavy clay soil. After the lecture, a member of the audience pointed out that this description exactly fitted the naked mole-rat and gave him Jarvis's address. This led to much fruitful collaboration, as a result of which it was found that there is a division of labour among mole-rats, as in social insects, even to the extent that there is only one breeding female per colony – the 'queen' mole-rat – the equivalent of a queen termite.

Ecological analogues

Unrelated species of plants and animals that occupy similar ecological niches in different zoogeographical regions of the world (see Chapter 4) often become remarkably alike as a result of parallel evolution. Consequently they are known as **ecological equivalents** or **analogues**. Some of the best known examples are the fennec fox of the Sahara and the American kit foxes, the kangaroo rats of North America and the Old World jerboas. The Australian thorny devil (*Moloch horridus*: Agamidae) closely resembles the horned lizards (*Phrynosoma*: Iguanidae) of North America in many ways and they all feed mainly on ants (Figure 3.10). Many species of cacti in the New World are strikingly similar in appearance and mode of life to the euphorbias and other succulent plants of the Old World.

3.10 Ecological analogues: (a) *Moloch horridus* (Agamidae), Australia; (b) *Phrynosoma platyrhinos* (Iguanidae), North America.

In this chapter we have touched on several aspects of the environment and its effects on plants and animals. Mention has also been made of some of the ways in which these interact with one another.

In subsequent chapters, other aspects of ecological complexity will be unravelled thereby revealing the underlying harmony and beauty of nature.

4 | TERRESTRIAL BIOMES

A space traveller, flying overland from pole to pole, would cross a number of recognisably different vegetational belts or biomes. These are especially well developed in the northern hemisphere because that is where most of the world's land mass lies. As he or she crossed the equator, the astronaut would see beneath an immense band of dark green rainforest. Much of this is being destroyed by human activities, as we shall see later, but the amount that remains is still impressive.

Further north, where the rainfall is less, the trees thin out and are replaced by grassy woodland savanna. In Africa, where the **savanna** is best developed, three belts are displayed, each with less precipitation (all of which falls in summer), fewer trees and more grasses than the preceding one. Finally the savanna merges into the desert wastes of the Sahara.

Around the Mediterranean Sea, the climate is characterised by winter rainfall. This supports a particular type of temperate forest scrub found throughout the world wherever the same conditions prevail. North-east of the Mediterranean, however, between the desert and the temperate forest biomes, lies a wide band of **steppe** grassland. This biome today comprises the grain belts of Asia and North America and the cattle ranches of Argentina. The soil is very rich. It is called **loess** and is composed of topsoil, blown for millennia from the sub-tropical deserts nearer to the equator, which have correspondingly been denuded of it.

As our astronaut continued his approach to the pole, he would pass over a wide area of deciduous forest, now almost entirely farmland, and then one of coniferous forest or **taiga** (its name in Siberia) which experiences exceptionally cold winters. Beyond the taiga lies the even colder **tundra** biome. Here there are virtually no trees. Only the surface layer of the soil melts in summer: deeper down, the ground is permanently frozen. Finally, the poles themselves are covered by ice packs and surrounded by snowlands. The seas support a rich fauna and flora, but terrestrial plants and animals are almost non-existent in polar regions.

Africa, Australia and New Zealand do not extend far enough to the south to have any taiga or Arctic tundra within their boundaries. The southernmost part of South America, however, has a cool temperate continental climate, the equivalent of the taiga in the northern hemisphere. The world's terrestrial biomes are, however, delineated more by their vegetation than directly by their climate (Figures 4.1, 4.2; Appendix II).

Continental drift

The nineteenth-century Scottish geologist Charles Lyell was probably the first person to point out that the present-day distribution of animals is the result of their past geological history. It is now generally recognised that animal groups originate in definite centres from which they disperse under the pressure of increasing population, competition for food and so on, until they are stopped by some geographical or climatic barrier. Not until the theory of **continental drift** was proposed by A.L. Wegener, early in the present century, were some of the stranger facts of animal distribution satisfactorily explained.

In the Permian period (250 to 225 million years ago) there was a single super continent Pangaea. This split into two – Laurasia in the north, Gondwana in the south – at the end of the Triassic period (160 million years ago). By this time, South America, Africa and India had broken free from Antarctica and, during the Cretaceous period (135 to 65 million years ago) they drifted far apart. The Indian plate moved northwards and collided with Asia, creating the Himalayas. The theory of **plate tectonics**, that the Earth's crust is divided into rock plates (oceanic, continental, or a combination of both) which move about the surface of the world at rates of 1 to 9 cm per year, has been proposed to explain how continental drift has taken place (Figure 4.3).

As a consequence of continental drift, the world can today be divided into nine **zoogeographical regions** (Figure 4.4) whose faunas are largely different, although a degree of migration has taken place between them. Some of the worst mistakes made by human colonists have been the introduction of viruses, bacteria, fungi, plants and animals from one zoogeographical region to another. Sometimes such introductions have been deliberate but more often they were accidental and due to ignorance. Notorious examples include the introduction of the prickly pear cactus and rabbit into Australia, of American grey squirrels and the Colorado beetle into Europe, not to mention the influenza virus and plague bacillus throughout human populations world-wide.

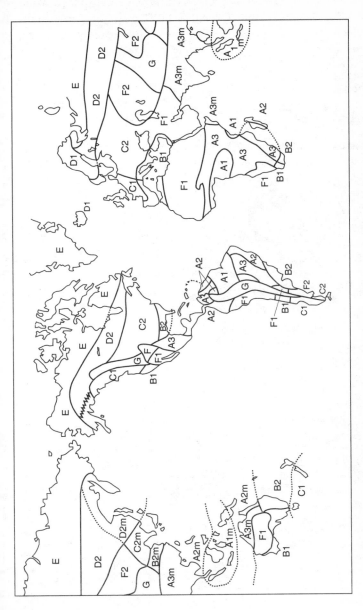

4.1 Distribution of climatic types and their vegetation (lettering as in Appendix II, m = monsoon).

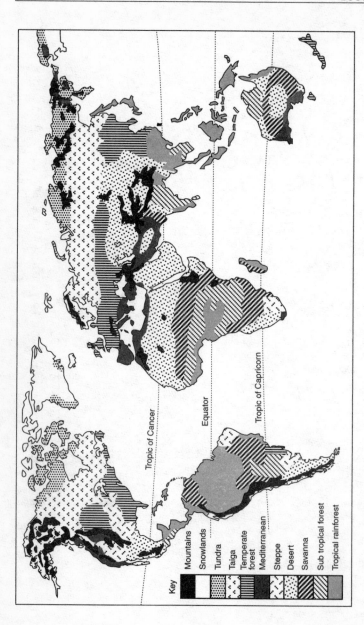

4.2 Vegetational biomes of the world.

Key

Mountains
Snowlands
Tundra
Taiga
Temperate forest
Mediterranean
Steppe
Desert
Savanna
Sub tropical forest
Tropical rainforest

Tropic of Cancer

Equator

Tropic of Capricorn

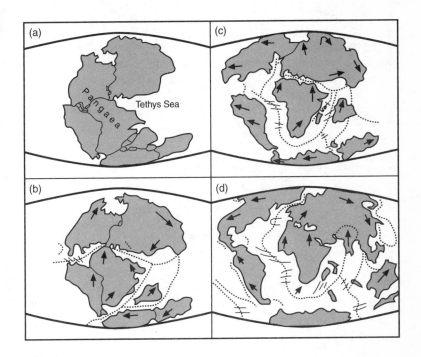

4.3 (a) The supercontinent (Pangaea) in the Permian period; (b) The southern and northern continents, Gondwana and Laurasia, separated by the Tethys Sea at the end of the Triassic, while South America, Africa and India had broken free from Antarctica; (c) By the end of the Cretaceous, South America and Africa had drifted well apart and the Indian plate was approaching Asia; (d) The Cenozoic (65 million years ago to present) distribution of the continents. Rifts and oceanic ridges from which the sea-floor spreading is occurring are shown by dotted lines, subduction zones by banded lines.

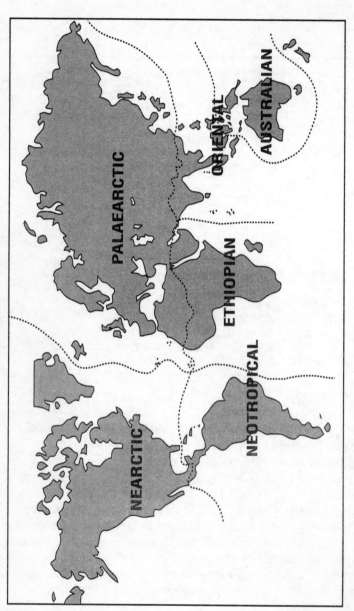

4.4 Zoogeographical regions of the world.

Tropical rainforest

A vast girdle of evergreen rainforest encircles the Earth between the tropics. It is bisected somewhat unequally by the equator so that rather more of its area lies in the northern than in the southern hemisphere. The largest continuous mass of rainforest is found in tropical America, with the huge Amazon basin as its centre. This extends from the Atlantic west to the lower slopes of the Andes and from southern Mexico into the region of the Gran Chaco. Tropical rainforest is often, incorrectly, referred to as 'jungle', an Indian word originally applied to the secondary forest which grows up after primary forest has been destroyed.

The central African rainforest extends throughout the Congo basin, throughout equatorial west and central Africa, with many breaks of savanna. Patches of rainforest are found on the Zambezi and rainforest is the natural **climax** vegetation of many of the islands of the Indian Ocean including the east coast of Madagascar, but very little of the original forest now remains in these places. By climax is meant the final and mature association of living organisms in a natural succession. A climax community is relatively stable and self-sustaining under the existing conditions of soil, climate and other environmental factors. If destroyed by natural causes, such as volcanic eruptions, hurricanes or natural fires, or by human activities, climax vegetation with its associated fauna is gradually replaced under natural conditions by a **succession** of communities over a period of time until, eventually, the stable climax community is restored.

In the eastern tropics, rainforest extends from western India and Sri Lanka, Burma, Thailand, Malaya, Borneo and New Guinea to the north coast of Australia. This tropical forest formation is the world's richest in numbers of plant species. Especially nearer the equator, tropical rainforest is the most luxuriant of all the Earth's biomes.

The conditions necessary for the production of tropical rainforest are like those in a hothouse. The mean annual temperature needs to be around 26.5 °C, rarely sinking below 21 °C or exceeding 32 °C. The moisture comes in the form of rain, with an annual minimum exceeding 150 cm – more effectively 200 cm – and distributed rather evenly throughout the year. Dry periods may be experienced in areas further from the equator, but they cannot be longer than two or three months at the most. If they are, evergreen rainforest is replaced by deciduous savanna.

A distinctive feature of tropical humid climates is the fact that the average daily range of temperature exceeds by several times the difference between the warmest and coolest months of the year. The rays of the Sun are never far from the vertical at midday, while the days and nights vary little in length between one month and the next.

At first glance the trees all look alike: most of them have smooth rather light-coloured bark and dark leathery leaves similar to those of laurel. Yet there are hundreds of species present. It is not unusual to find more than 25 different species of tree over 30 cm in diameter growing in a single hectare of land. In Britain you would probably find only two or three species in a hectare of woodland while in the Appalachian forests of the United States – probably the richest of any temperate forest – you would be lucky to find more than a dozen.

Even more surprising are the botanical relationships of rainforest trees. Many of the largest belong to families that in temperate regions include mainly small, soft-stemmed plants. Many of them are relatives of the common European violet or North American milkwort. **Buttresses** which radiate from their bases are a striking feature of many of the largest trees (Figure 4.5). These are thin triangular plates of hard wood that form in the angles between the trunks and horizontal roots running near the surface of the ground. There are usually about three or four but there may be up to ten. They provide support for the trees where the soil is thin, making long tap roots unnecessary and thereby saving the expenditure of energy on producing wood.

The main vegetative components of tropical rainforest are:

1 **Forest trees**. These form the roof or **canopy** in which most of the insects and birds live. As they push upwards, competing for the sunlight, they form a series of indistinct layers, each a miniature life zone in which animals feed and may pass their entire lives. There are usually from three to five such layers in the **stratification** of mature tropical rainforest. Below the canopy is a middle layer formed of smaller trees where crowns do not meet. The next layer is composed of woody and herbaceous shrubs. Finally there is a ground layer of non-woody herbs and tree seedlings (Figure 4.5). Very little light reaches this layer but, if one of the canopy trees should be felled or blown over in a storm, intense competition between the seedlings takes place. Eventually the hole in the canopy will be filled by another majestic giant.

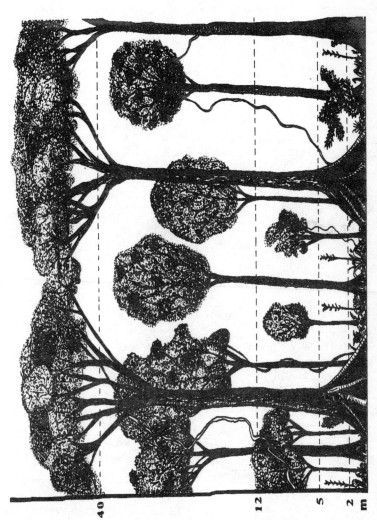

4.5 Rainforest stratification, showing five layers of vegetation.

2 **Herbs** occur wherever the canopy is not too dense. Their stems tend to be sappy and brittle and, in some cases, the stem is supported at the base by aerial 'prop' roots. In contrast with the monotonous uniformity of the trees and shrubs, the herbs of the rainforest have leaves with a variegated pattern of white or pale green but the flowers are usually inconspicuous. In a few species the leaves have a velvety surface.

3 **Climbers**. Vines or lianas, thin as ropes or as thick as a man's thigh, vanish like cables into the mass of foliage overhead. They are especially abundant on river banks and where the canopy is thinner. Rainforest climbers fall into two groups: large, woody lianas which reach up to the canopy and are therefore exposed to sunlight when adult, and much smaller herbaceous forms which seldom emerge from the shade of the undergrowth. For both of these, climbing on other plants provides a quick and economical method of reaching towards the light.

4 **Stranglers** form one of the most remarkable groups of tropical rainforest plants and have no equivalents in the temperate regions of the globe. They begin their lives as **epiphytes** (see below), but later send roots down to the soil. Eventually they become independent, often killing the trees that originally supported them. Strangling figs (*Ficus*) are abundant in the African, Indo-Malaysian and Australian rainforests. In South America the most important genus of stranglers, *Clusia*, is likewise represented by numerous species.

5 **Epiphytes** grow on the trunks and branches, and even on the leaves of trees, shrubs and lianas. In closed forest, the epiphyte habitat provides the only niche available for small plants that have relatively high demands for light. Their water supply is precarious and their roots lack natural soil. Many are so constructed, however, that they accumulate among their roots a substitute soil derived from the dead remains of other plants and often collected by ants. They depend upon their host plants solely for mechanical support: only mistletoes (Loranthaceae) (Chapter 10) are parasitic as well as being saprophytic (see below).

6 **Saprophytes**. These plants absorb soluble organic nutrients from decomposing plant or animal matter, dung and so on. They live either on the forest floor or between the buttresses of trees where dead leaves tend to accumulate. Saprophytes include bacteria, fungi and some higher plants such as orchids and gentians. Except for some of the orchids, they tend to be inconspicuous and are easily overlooked.

7 **Parasites** are organisms, usually relatively small, that live on others (their **hosts**) from which they obtain food and shelter (see Chapter 10). The vegetative parasites of tropical rainforest are either root-parasites or arboreal epiphytes belonging to the family Loranthaceae. Only two families of root parasites, the Balanophoraceae and Rafflesiaceae, are represented in rainforest. The latter includes the Indonesian *Rafflesia arnoldii*, which has the largest flowers of any known plant. Discovered in 1818, its blossoms may attain a diameter of 1.4 m. These are the visible part of the plant and lie directly on the ground. Only small, thin suckers penetrate the roots of lianas which are the host plants.

Fauna

The fauna of tropical rainforest reflects the stratification of the vegetation. The canopy of leaves and flowers is inhabited by innumerable insects, spiders and other small animals that are found at ground level in other biomes. Because seasons are absent and fruit is obtainable throughout the year, rainforest can support fruit-eating animals such as chimpanzees, fruit-bats and parrots which would be quite unable to find a regular supply of their favourite food anywhere else in the world. Toucans (Ramphastidae) in the New World and hornbills (Bucerotidae) in the Old World both exploit the perannual availability of fruit in tropical forests. They are unrelated, but are ecological analogues. Their bills are superficially similar and enable them to reach fruit on thin branches that would not support their weight (Figure 4.6.).

The neotropical rainforest in particular is the great metropolis of tree-living termites, an important source of food for many animals. Termite nests are found in all strata of the rainforest. They are made by cementing together particles of soil and wood and are often connected to the ground by covered passages through which the termites travel. Termites are

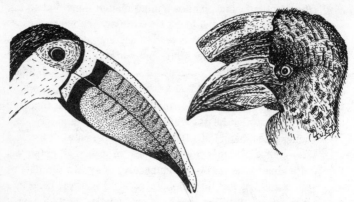

4.6 Beaks of toucan (left) and hornbill (right) showing parallel adaptations for reaching fruit on thin branches.

especially important in the ecology of the forest because their wood-eating habits hasten the decay of fallen trees. Their role in the production of humus parallels that of earthworms in temperate biomes.

Anyone who comes fresh to the rainforest may well be disappointed at the apparent paucity of animal life there. This is partly because the animals are dwarfed by the luxuriance of the vegetation and partly because the most abundant and brightly coloured species live in the upper reaches of the trees. In general, the numbers of soil-dwelling invertebrates tend to be fewer in the wet tropics and their sizes larger than those of their counterparts in temperate forests. Most mammals are adapted for arboreal life, while ground-living species are usually small, stealthy forms that wind their way unobtrusively through the vegetation. Only the forest elephant moves by sheer strength, blazing trails that are subsequently made use of by smaller species including hippopotamuses, rhinos, buffaloes, pigs and carnivores such as leopards.

The number of species of larger mammals is much smaller than in open savanna. Their sizes are also less than those of their relatives outside the rainforest. Forest elephants (*Loxodonta africana cyclotis*) are smaller than bush elephants (*L.africana africana*), forest buffaloes are smaller than the plains subspecies and the same applies to leopards. The royal antelope is the smallest ruminant in the world and many other dwarf antelopes of the rainforest are not much larger. The bongo (*Boocerus euryceros*) is exceptional in its large size.

Savanna

Savanna is a much less complex biome than rainforest. Savanna woodlands are often found where the dry season is longer and the rainfall less heavy than in rainforest. They separate the Earth's belts of equatorial and tropical forest from its desert regions. The trees are scattered and grade into tropical grasslands before they peter out completely as the aridity increases. There are two fundamental types of tropical climate – marine and continental (Appendix II). The former does not show a pronounced dry season and is restricted to narrow strips on the eastern margins of the continental masses. Westward, however, rainfall decreases rapidly and in this direction the forest passes gradually into savanna. The savanna biome experiences a long dry season and summer rains – a so-called **monsoon** climate (Figures 4.1, 4.2).

Savanna vegetation is found under a variety of climatic conditions raging from annual summer rainfall of 50 cm with seven or eight months of drought up to about 255 cm annual precipitation with negligible drought periods. Short grass savanna predominates where there is less than 90 cm annually. The Africa savanna is the best developed. It can be subdivided into a number of distinct regions. The most northerly of these, which grades into the Sahara, is known as the **Sahel**. The rainfall here is about 25 to 50 cm, concentrated in four or five months of the year. The vegetation consists mostly of small, scattered thorny trees and tufts of short grass.

Further to the south lies **Sudan** savanna. Here the trees are larger, the herb stratum continuous and dominated by grasses – but these are now 1.0 to 1.5 m high. Grass fires are fierce, and more frequent than in the Sahel. The annual rainfall is in the region of 50 to 100 cm and the dry season lasts from October to April. Adjoining the northern border of the rainforest belt lies **Guinea** savanna. This is relatively moist, with precipitation of 100 to 150 cm per year, nearly all of which falls in seven or eight months. The trees are larger still and the woodland much denser than further north.

Guinea savanna, like **miombo** savanna (its counterpart to the south of the equator), would probably be thick seasonal forest if left to itself, as this is probably the natural climax. Its floral composition would, however, differ from that of evergreen rainforest because it experiences less precipitation and a longer dry season. The climax vegetation of Sudan and Sahel vegetation is probably also seasonal forest of one kind or another.

Formation of savanna

The destruction of African forest and the development of savanna doubtless began when humans first acquired the use of fire. This may be why savanna is better developed in Africa north of the equator, where *Homo sapiens* evolved, than it is anywhere else in the world. Fire is an essential tool in shifting cultivation and is responsible for the maintenance of savanna. Although fires must naturally occur from time to time, deliberate firing by human beings has a far greater effect upon the vegetation. This is because artificial fires cover the same ground more frequently than do natural fires. Moreover, they are not associated with thunderstorms, the rain from which may quench the fires that lightning has started.

Whereas the fauna of rainforest is remarkable, chiefly on account of its extraordinary wealth and variety of species, animal life in savanna is characterised by larger numbers but fewer species. Insects are often present in vast swarms – especially locusts and grasshoppers (Orthoptera), termites (Isoptera) and ants (Hymenoptera). Birds are common too because food is plentiful and their mobility enables them to avoid conditions that are temporarily unfavourable. Many species are migratory. The dominant forms are ground living species such as ostriches, emus and rheas.

The mammals of savanna, like those of steppe grassland (see below), tend either to be large cursorial froms, such as buffaloes and bison, antelopes and zebras, or small burrowing insectivores and rodents. In Australasia these groups are represented by marsupials such as kangaroos and wallabies which show parallel evolution in many respects with placental mammals.

Desert

Beyond the limits of the swing of the equatorial rainfall belt, at the latitudes in which trade winds blow throughout the year, lie the world's greatest deserts. Here the annual precipitation is less than 25.5 cm. Hot deserts, such as the Sahara and Kalahari, have no cold season but, in the so-called 'cold deserts', like the Gobi and Great Basin, one or more of the winter months has a mean temperature below 6 °C. Deserts are not necessarily very hot, nor do they always consist of vast expanses of dunes. The characteristics common to them all are their aridity and the extremes of temperature to which they are subject.

Most desert and semi-desert regions support a little vegetation. The least amount of plant life is found in areas of **hammada** or denuded rock. Where these are traversed by the beds of **wadis** or **arroyos** (water courses that are dry for most of the year) there may be a few shrubs. The spacing of desert plants reduces competition for scarce sources of water.

Desert organisms are adapted to their harsh environment, not just by a single character, but by a combination of factors that operate simultaneously. These can be summarised as follows:

1 Evasion of drought and heat by completing their life cycles before the onset of seasonal stressful conditions;

2 Avoidance and escape from heat and drought. In the case of plants this is by the possession of very long roots that reach the water table. Most small animals retreat during the day into burrows and shelters where the **microclimate** (see below) is less harsh than outside;

3 Tolerance of heat and drought by physiological means;

4 Habitat selection.

Beyond the edges of true desert are shrub-steppe lands, such as the *Acacia* desert scrub which lies south of the Sahara and merges with the Sahel savanna. Acacia and, in America, mesquite (*Prosopis*) trees have roots that can reach a depth of up to 50 m. Succulent plants, such as cacti and agaves, store water in roots, stems or leaves. The barrel cactus (*Ferocactus wislizeni*) stores so much that it has been used as an emergency source of drinking water by American Indians, and other inhabitants of the North American deserts.

Fauna

The fauna of the Sahara is an extension of that of the Sahel in the south and of the Mediterranean biome in the north. As in other deserts, bristle-tails (Lepismatidae), termites, grasshoppers, ants and beetles – especially beetles of the family Tenebrionidae – are particularly successful desert insects. They support a number of arachnid predators of which scorpions and camel-spiders (Solifugae) are dominant members. Day active lizards and burrowing nocturnal rodents such as jerboas and kangaroo rats are probably the most successful of desert vertebrates but many other groups are represented in the faunas of the world's deserts. Even large desert animals, such as camels, gazelles and other antelopes, utilise shade as much as possible. In addition to their physiological adaptations, the long limbs increase surface to volume ratio, thereby assisting cooling. The backs of ostriches and camels are shaded by feathers and hairs respectively, while the flanks which are not exposed to direct sunlight are not insulated (Figure 4.7).

Mediterranean scrub

Whereas the subtropical deserts have monsoon climates with summer rain, regions with Mediterranean climates, as already mentioned, receive their precipitations mainly in winter. In addition to the **maquis** surrounding the Mediterranean Sea, Mediterranean climates supporting **chaparral** evergreen oak scrub vegetation are found in California. Mediterranean climates also occur in central Chile as well as on the southern coasts of Australia and South Africa. Fire plays an important role in the formation of Mediterranean as well as of the wooded savanna ecosystems and should perhaps be regarded as a natural climatic factor.

Steppe

Grasslands occupy the interiors of the continents in temperate regions where the summers are hot, the winters cold and there is low annual rainfall. Only on the shores of lakes and along the banks of rivers is there usually sufficient moisture for trees to grow. Everywhere else the land is covered with a rolling carpet of short grass. The world's largest area of

---

4.7 Vertebrate animals of the desert: (a) Thorny devil (*Moloch horridus*) (15 cm); (b) Horned viper (*Cerastes cerastes*) (30 cm); (c) Sandgrouse (*Pterocles*) (30 cm); (d) Pratincole (*Glareola*) (25 cm); (e) Ostrich (*Struthio camelus*) (240 cm); (f) Jerboa (*Jaculus*) (15 cm); (g) Fennec fox (*Fennecus zerda*) (30 cm); (h) Dorcas gazelle (*Gazella dorcas*) (50 cm); (i) Arabian oryx (*Oryx leucoryx*) (100 cm). (Drawings not to scale.)

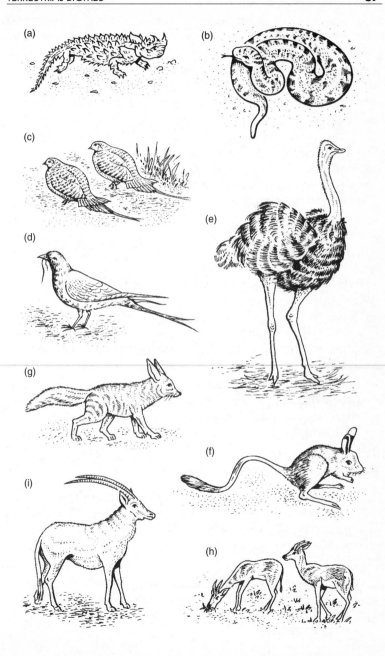

temperate grassland is the steppe of Europe and Asia, a vast plain stretching from Hungary through southern Russia to China in the east. Northward, it merges with deciduous or coniferous forest: to the south it is bordered by the Black Sea, the Caspian Sea and the deserts of Central Asia. The steppes and prairies of North America, now the grain belt of the continent, occupy two-thirds of the United States and much of Canada.

For climatic reasons, temperate steppe grassland is a biome somewhat adverse to plant growth. In contrast, there is a brief season of luxuriant growth in savanna at the time of the rains. The dominant species of the Eurasian steppes is the meadow grass (*Poa pratensis*). This has been introduced into North America, where it is known as Kentucky blue grass. It is popular in horse-raising areas as a staple feed.

The fauna of steppe and other grasslands appears to have few, if any, elements peculiar to itself. Almost all of its species also inhabit either the forests to the north or the deserts to the south. The dominant mammals are rodents and social ungulates. A century ago, the bison was the chief grazing animal in central North America but, within a few years, it was entirely replaced by cattle, sheep and other kinds of farming. The 'buffalo bird' (*Molothrus ater*) remained, however, as the 'cow bird' of modern pastures. Characteristic of the Asian steppes are the saiga antelope, which almost experienced a fate similar to that of the bison, and wild asses.

Because the bulk of the land mass of the world lies in the northern hemisphere, there is comparatively little grassland in the southern hemisphere (Figure 4.2). Here the steppes of the north are represented by the **pampas** of eastern Argentina, the Patagonian semidesert and the tussock grasslands of South Island, New Zealand.

Temperate forest

Temperate forest regions are those in which most of the readers of this book probably reside. Because they have been so profoundly modified by farming, logging and other human activities, however, very little of this biome now remains in its natural state. The three main types of temperate forest are as follows:

1 **Temperate deciduous forest** which originally covered eastern North America, most of Europe, and parts of Asia, Japan, Australia and South America; but it has been very much reduced;

    2 **Moist temperate coniferous forest** found in western North
      America from California to Alaska and in the Mississippi
      delta (it is quite distinct from taiga – see below). The
      humidity is high and precipitation often supplemented by
      fog. Conifers, such as redwoods (*Sequoia*) and spruces
      (*Picea*) dominate;

    3 **Broad-leaved evergreen forest** which is found where
      moisture is high and differences in temperature between
      summer and winter are less than in deciduous forest. This
      type of vegetation is characteristic of central and southern
      Japan and of Florida. Live oaks (*Quercus virgineana*),
      magnolias, hollies, bays, and sabal palms (*Sabal palmetto*)
      are typical trees.

The temperate forest biome is packed with delightful and unexpected variations. Meadows are common, as are lakes and ponds (*see* Chapter 5). If shallow, these often become dense thickets of willows. On moderate slopes there may be subalpine forest (see below) containing many conifers and grading into the taiga of the following section. **Rendzina** soils are typical of chalkland. They are formed by weathering of the underlying parent limestone. They support a sward rich in plant species, mainly grasses and regions of shrubs and bushes. Large areas of the chalk downs of Europe have for centuries been grazed by rabbits and sheep which, by continual tramping, nibbling of the vegetation and killing the seedlings of shrubs and trees, have arrested the development of the normal succession. By far the most widespread climax of succession is beech woodland although a sub-climax of ash or yew is often attained first.

Over wide areas of podsol in western and north-western Europe, cool temperate forest is replaced by heather moors in which ling heather (*Calluna vulgaris*) is the dominant species, often mixed with *Erica*, related heaths and the crowberry (*Empetrum nigrum*). Although of a different family than the heaths, crowberries bear a striking resemblance to cranberries, bilberries, cowberries and so on.

Conditions of life are very different in forest than they are in open habitats. The inhabitants of temperate forest do not show the numbers and diversity seen in tropical rainforest, but they enjoy a greater range of environmental adaptations than are to be found in grassland. Non-arboreal mammals include mice, hedgehogs and badgers. Many of these hibernate in winter, but shrews do not hibernate. This is because they have such a high metabolic rate that they must eat continuously in order to survive. Their metabolism drops when they sleep but not enough to allow them to take long periods of rest. Other charcteristic mammals of temperate forest are red deer, roe deer, wild boar, foxes, wild cats, martens and the lynx. Squirrels are arboreal.

The temperate forest biome has a rich fauna of bats and birds. Woodpeckers, nuthatches, warblers, hawks and owls find their food even in dense forest. Most insectivorous birds either feed on seeds during the winter, or else migrate to regions where insects remain active. Tits and tree-creepers, however, remain in deciduous forest throughout the year and survive in winter by finding the larvae and pupae of insects. Seasonal rhythms and breeding cycles are adapted to the **phenology** or annually recurring climatic conditions of the biome.

Taiga

Taiga is able to exist in regions where the growing season is too short to support deciduous woodland. Because their leaves do not fall but survive throughout the winter, coniferous trees are ready to begin photosynthesis without delay, as soon as temperatures become favourable. Moreover, the coniferous type of fruiting has the advantage that it is pollinated one year and dispersed the next, whereas deciduous trees have to complete the process within a single season. The number of months with temperatures above the threshold necessary for growth is the most significant factor controlling forest types.

The Siberian taiga is the largest in the world. It extends from the Ural Mountains to the Pacific Ocean, a distance of some 5800 km. In contrast to tropical rainforest or even temperate forest, the trees of the taiga belong to comparatively few species. They are **xerophytes**, plants that are adapted to dry conditions. They grow in soil that is physiologically dry in winter because the water in it is frozen and are exposed to bitter, desiccating, winds throughout much of the year. The prolonged cold of the continental winter is a severe restriction on both flora and fauna. The main types of taiga are:

1 **Mixed coniferous forest** dominated by spruce, fir, pine and larch;

2 **Open taiga**, where forest is sparse and trees scattered;

3 **Lake forest** around the Great Lakes of North America. This climax is dominated by white pine, Norway pine and hemlock.

The mammals of the taiga include wolves, bears, wolverines, badgers, lynxes, otters, stoats, elks, mooses and rodents. Most bird species are migratory. Thrushes, finches and buntings are especially numerous, while crossbills are completely adapted to life in coniferous forest. They live in the upper branches of the trees like little parrots, which they resemble somewhat in their bright plumage. Their beaks are specially modified to split fir cones. The upper and lower mandibles are crossed so that their tips overlap (Figure 4.8). The insect life of the taiga is surprisingly rich. Coniferous trees are attacked by bark beetles, among the most serious enemies the forester has to contend with. Pine sawflies, wood wasps, moths and flies have all been able to adapt successfully to the climatic hardships of the taiga.

4.8 Head of crossbill showing adaptation of the beak to split fir cones.

Tundra and snowlands

Arctic climates are of two types:

1 **Tundra** climates with a summer, however short, above freezing;
2 **Polar** or climates of perpetual frost in which the growth of vegetation is impossible.

Tundra, a word of Finnish origin, means an open, forestless stretch of country. It is applied to the biome lying north of the taiga but which nevertheless thaws in summer. Patches of stunted coniferous forest in the valleys of rivers such as the Lena and Yenisei represent outliers of the taiga. The inequality of the length of day and night is so great that the diurnal range of temperature is insignificant. The difference between summer and winter is all that matters. Although it may seem paradoxical, the swampy tundra has much in common with hot deserts. For, while deserts are physically dry, the tundra is physiologically dry because water is frozen and inaccessible to living organisms for most of the year.

Polar climates are excessively cold because the rays of the sun strike the surface of the land at such an oblique angle that they are unable to warm it effectively. The Antarctic, with its great land mass and high mountains, is even colder than the Arctic. Although precipitation is meagre, the amount of evaporation is so low that great permanent fields of snow and ice have accumulated. If these melt in consequence of the greenhouse effect (Chapters 3 and 11), much of human civilisation may be threatened.

Only a handful of hardy plant species can survive in the tundra. In response to the extremely short growing season, the production of seeds has generally been discarded in favour of vegetative reproduction. Plants grow favourably until nipped by the winter cold. Dwarf birches, willows and ling form a characteristic element of the vegetation; but much of the tundra overlies deep deposits of sphagnum which result in part from the failure of dead plants to decompose at low temperatures.

The most striking mammals of the tundra are caribou and wolves, lemmings, Arctic hares, foxes and stoats. Caribou are migratory and so do not overgraze the slow-growing lichens on which they feed, although they move in enormous herds. In parts of Newfoundland, the rocks are worn away to a depth of half a metre by the thousands of hooves that have passed across them over countless decades of migration. When domesticated reindeer were introduced into Alaska at the end of the nineteenth century, their numbers increased rapidly and then declined catastrophically. The relatively sedentary habits of these domesticated caribou had led to the destruction of their food supplies.

Birds are the most conspicuous animals of the tundra in summer, but only the hardiest species winter in the north. Most arrive at the beginning of summer and concentrate on establishing territories, courtship and mating. When the thaw sets in, vast swarms of mosquitoes, blackflies and other insects provide abundant food both for adult birds and their nestlings, which must be ready to migrate south before the winter sets in.

Mountains

On account of the low temperatures, trees do not grow at very high altitudes. The region above the timber line is known as the **Alpine zone** in all parts of the world. It is in many ways similar to the Arctic regions discussed above. There are certain differences, however. Atmospheric pressure is lower at high altitudes and the air is thin. Consequently, insolation is powerful on mountain tops – in contrast to Arctic and Antarctic snowlands where the Sun's rays are strongly filtered as they pass through the atmosphere. Winds reach high speed on mountains because frictional drag with the Earth's surface is reduced. Consequently evaporation is increased.

The number of floral and faunal zones on a high mountain is greatest in the tropics since its base may be in tropical forest and its top above the snowline. Every such mountain shows four or five belts or zones whose width is proportional to the steepness of the slope:

1 **Tropical zone** where the climate is hot and moist or dry according to locality. Vegetation is usually evergreen;

2 **Warm temperate zone**. Here the difference between summer and winter begins to be marked and the nights cool. Vegetation is chiefly evergreen;

3 **Cool temperate zone**. This often coincides with the cloud level. The winters are well marked and deciduous trees lose their leaves at this time;

4 **Alpine zone**. Characterised by grassy slopes and tundra vegetation. Higher up the grass is replaced by moss and lichens;

5 **Arctic** or **nival zone**. The lower limit of this is near the permanent snow line. Only a few hardy flowering plants are found, with lichens encrusting bare rock surfaces.

The Alpine fauna is, in many ways, similar to that of the tundra. Pronounced pigmentation of the body is one of the most striking characteristics of most high-altitude insects as it is of insects in Artic regions. Mountain-dwelling mammals need to be sure footed, like the Nubian ibex which can scale almost sheer rock faces in the mountains of

Arabia and North Africa. At high altitudes, growth is severely restricted to the summer months and seasonal rhythms of reproductive activity are extremely well marked. Prolonged hibernation takes place under snow cover and a correspondingly short period of rapid development during the brief summer.

Caves

In some ways the ecology of caves can be considered as the ecology of extremes. Caves are dark, humid and lacking daily and seasonal cycles of temperature. The eyes of cave animals are often reduced or absent, their greatly enlarged appendages compensating for the lack of visual senses in complete darkness. The cave environment is extremely stable and the populations of animals that inhabit them are relatively steady in size. The number of species found in many cave communities is quite small and ecological analogues frequently occur in many different cave systems. This is not surprising, considering that over 2300 separate caves are known in the state of Virginia alone. Study of the ecology of caves has provided valuable information about genetics and adaptation, sensory compensation, metabolic economy and population genetics. There is insufficient space to discuss these matters further here.

Microhabitats

In the world's most adverse environments, both plants and animals have evolved mechanisms for avoiding drought and extremes of temperatures, as well as for resisting them. Seeds, tubers and rhizomes buried in the soil are not exposed to the excessive temperatures of the desert, while dormant seeds can often resist them. Even when active, some animals are able to withstand surprisingly high or low temperatures, although the measurements may sometimes be misleading. This is because **microhabitats**, in which conditions are less extreme than elsewhere in the environment, are actively sought out. Although the temperature in the water of a hot spring may be almost boiling, few of the insects and fishes that live in it can tolerate more than 40 to 50 °C for long. The answer to this apparent paradox is that they lurk near the surface film and at the edges of the spring, microhabitats in which the water is considerably cooler. A similar explanation applies to many desert animals that survive by avoiding exposure to extremes of temperature during the day and emerging from their burrows and retreats only during the night. For instance, jerboas and kangaroo rats are able to exist on a diet of dry seeds, without any water to drink, in the world's hottest deserts. They only emerge from their holes at night and escape from the daytime heat by hiding underground.

Epiphytes play an important role as microenvironments for small animals in the tropical rainforest ecosystem. The spaces between their leaves are often inhabited by a vast array of insect larvae, planarians, earthworms, termites, grasshoppers, earwigs, ants, scorpions, spiders, centipedes, millipedes, snails, treefrogs, lizards, snakes and so on.

These are merely a few striking examples of the innumerable microhabitats inhabited by plants and animals throughout the world. A microhabitat can be defined as a self-contained entity which reflects in miniature the ecological balance of living organisms in general. Indeed, microecology is a subject as vast as almost any other aspect of ecological science and merits a book to itself.

Only the main terrestrial biomes of the planet have been discussed in this chapter, but enough has been said to indicate that order, imposed primarily by climate, underlies the complexity of the soils, vegetation and fauna of the Earth.

5 | AQUATIC BIOMES

The sea covers more than 70 per cent of the Earth's surface while the amount occupied by inland waters, fresh or brackish, is by no means negligible. The producers in the food chains of both oceans and large lakes away from the shore lines are phytoplankton consisting of cyanobacteria and photosynthetising Protista such as diatoms, dinoflagellates and coccolithopores. This is a group of flagellates with shells composed of a small number of calcareous plates (Figure 5.1).

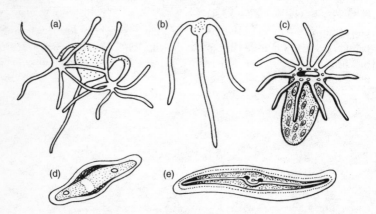

5.1 Examples of marine phytoplankton: (a) and (b) Dinoflagellates; (c) Coccolithophore; (d) and (e) Diatoms. (Not to scale.)

The primary consumers in aquatic food webs are the smallest members of the zooplankton – copepods in fresh water and, in the sea, arrow worms (Chaetognatha). The greater the salt content of the water, the greater is its buoyancy and the easier it is for very small organisms to float in it. Consequently, marine plankton is almost invariably richer than fresh water plankton. Organisms that spend their entire lives drifting about in the waters of lakes and seas are said to be **pelagic** and the pelagic zone of the open sea constitutes about 90 per cent of its area.

Oceanic currents and the circulation of nutrients

The open waters of the ocean constitute the pelagic zone. Within this zone, there are huge currents in which water is continually circulating. One of these currents is the **Gulf Stream**. This originates in the Gulf of Mexico. It emerges through the Straits of Florida and, as a result of the continually blowing north-east trade winds, moves in a north-easterly direction across the Atlantic Ocean north of the equator. It is deflected even more to the east by the rotation of the Earth and by the time it has reached 40°N it is flowing almost due east. Near the Labrador coast it meets vast masses of drifting ice in the polar current flowing from the Arctic Ocean. These massive ice floes cool the surface waters which sink, only to be replaced by warmer waters from below. These are rich in nutrients, especially phosphates and nitrates, hence the richness of plankton and therefore of marine life generally in the far North Atlantic where the world's greatest fisheries are located.

In the South Atlantic the circulation is slightly different on account of the configuration of the land masses. Off the coast of south-west Africa, the cold **Benguela** current is responsible for the Kalahari–Namib desert. In the Pacific, too, there is a somewhat similar system of oceanic currents. The **Kurashio** or Japan current corresponds to the Gulf Stream, while the cold **Humboldt** current flowing along the coast of South America is the cause of the Atacama–Peruvian desert (Figure 5.2). The cool waters of these currents react with the warm coastal air above them to engender dense blankets of fog. These trap moisture at sea and ground level, preventing moist air from rising to form rain cloud. Life in these extremely arid deserts depends almost entirely upon the condensation of the fog.

The open sea

Life in the pelagic zone consists of drifting plankton and animals higher in the food web that depend upon it for food. The zone is, however, poor in nutrients and, therefore, in both primary and secondary productivity.

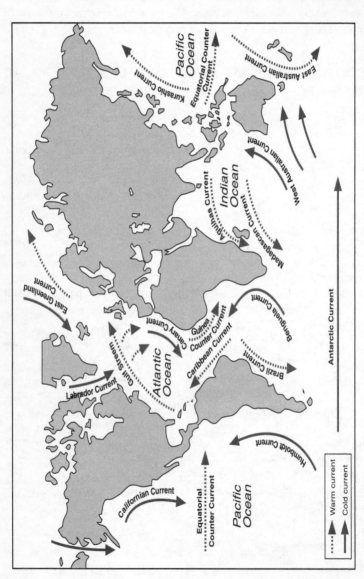

5.2 Major ocean currents of the world. Warmer currents are indicated by broken lines.

Nevertheless, the upwelling of waters from below, which are richer in nutrients, supports the North Atlantic fisheries and the summer blooms of the Antarctic waters. These blooms are sufficient to support fin and blue whales. The latter are the largest animals alive today and may reach a length over 33 m. The heaviest recorded, a female 27.6 m long, weighed 190 tonnes. Since killer whales, only 9 m in length and weighing perhaps 7 tonnes, have been known to eat several porpoises, dolphins or seals, in one meal, it is obvious that a whale the size of a blue whale or 'rorqual' would soon 'eat itself out of house and home' were it not to feed on very much smaller animals that can reproduce and grow extremely quickly, as previously mentioned. Baleen whales, manta rays, whale sharks and basking sharks are all so huge that they have to be **filter feeders**, eating small crustaceans. The most important of these are krill. Although they reach about 6 cm in length and dominate the zooplankton of the Southern Ocean, possibly forming up to half its entire biomass, krill have to be filtered from the sea water. This is achieved by means of the whalebone or baleen plates of the rorquals and other whalebone whales and the fringes of long slender gill-rakers which adorn the branchial arches of the rays and sharks.

Nekton

Marine animals which are capable of swimming powerfully and at speeds that make them independent of ocean currents, such as squids, fishes and whales, are known collectively as **nekton**. By far the most important components of the nekton are fishes. Even though their numbers may not be large, pelagic fish play an important part in the ecology of the sea. They produce more than half of all fish caught for human consumption. Many fishes aggregate in 'schools' which may vary from a few individuals to enormous shoals. Herring schools occupying over 75 square kilometres (km²) have been seen in the North Sea. Fishes in schools have a better chance of survival than they would if they swam alone. Predators are more likely to encounter one of many solitary individuals than to come across a single school. Furthermore, the larger the school, the less is the probability of any individual fish being eaten.

Birds and mammals of the nekton can be divided into two groups:

1 Those that come ashore to breed – penguins, auks, puffins, sea otters, sea lions and seals;

2 Whales which spend their entire lives at sea.

The latter are divided into two families, the whalebone whales (Mysticeti) and the toothed whales (Odontoceti). The latter are tertiary consumers and range from top predators such as the large sperm whale to killer whales, porpoises and dolphins. Marine mammals also include sea cows and manatees, both of which are primary vegetarian consumers.

A unique drifting ecosystem is found on the surface of the Sargasso Sea in the North Atlantic east of Florida. This is a habitat for drifting sea weed consisting of two species of brown algae, *Sargassum natans* and *S.fluitans*. These algae normally live in the shallow waters of the tropical Atlantic coasts of America but, when detached by wave action, they float with the aid of air-filled bladders. Trapped at the surface of an immense whirlpool, they continue to live and grow for centuries, although they are unable to reproduce. Among these floating weeds live a variety of animals including hydrozoans, sea anemones, polychaete worms, shrimps, crabs, snails and fishes – several of which are not found elsewhere.

Vertical migration

Vertical daily movements are a characteristic feature of the behaviour of many free-swimming planktonic organisms in both salt and fresh waters. In general, strong sunlight is avoided, each species showing a preference for a certain light intensity. For this reason, few organisms are to be found in the surface layers of the water during the day. At dusk, however, they tend to swim upwards but, when all is dark, they scatter again. Over the years 1925–34, Wing Commander F.S. Russell carried out an enormous amount of work on the distribution of many planktonic animals in the area of Plymouth, Devon. He confirmed previous observations to the effect that, in general, few zooplankton are found where the phytoplankton is most dense. The reason for this is still not absolutely clear. One factor in the relationship could be that where animals are present they graze the crop of phytoplankton so that it is greatly reduced. Conversely, the phytoplankton multiplies where the zooplankton is scarce. Herring and other fishes are known to avoid areas of dense phytoplankton. In the light of this A.C. Hardy and E.R. Gunter in 1935 proposed a hypothesis of **animal exclusion**. They suggested that zooplankton feed only for short periods in zones of dense phytoplankton – possibly because of its antibiotic effect. This has been neither proved nor disproved. The patchy distribution of plankton is probably due to a great variety of causes. Nutritive salts carried into sunlit water by upwelling may result in the growth of dense patches of phytoplankton which affect the zooplankton indirectly. The migration of plankton has also been studied in fresh as well as salt water and we shall return to it later.

As we have seen, the concentration of nutrients is low in oceanic waters. Nevertheless the top millimetre of the ocean plays an important role in the global regulation of carbon dioxide. In the absence of vertical mixing (except in just a few regions) the deep waters, which constitute about 60 per cent of the ocean, remain permanently near 3 °C. Most of the plankton lives above in the sunlit waters between the surface and a depth of 75 to 200 m. The organisms that inhabit the pelagic zone at depths below this are completely dependent on the dead organisms that rain down from the upper regions. They are therefore wholly heterotropic. In deeper waters many animals have reduced vision as do cave dwellers. Others have evolved eyes that are highly sensitive to the light produced by bioluminescent forms.

Life on the sea bed

The fauna at the bottom of the sea is much richer in species than are the pelagic flora and fauna combined. While some 3000 pelagic species are known, nearly 160 000 species live on the sea bed itself. The majority of these occur at depths of less than 200 m, however, and there are many more of them in tropical waters than in cold seas. Temperature is an important environmental factor and the influence of warm oceanic currents such as the Gulf Stream and Kurashio current is extremely influential on the distribution of seashore plants and animals. In coastal areas, numbers decrease rapidly with depth.

Organisms that live on the bottom of the sea can be subdivided into two groups; the **epiflora** and **epifauna** (which are found on the surface of the sea bed or on rocks, stones, shells, seaweeds and so on) and the **infauna**. The latter consists of animals which live buried in sand, mud, or deposits of silt. Examples of both groups are to be seen in the ecosystems described below.

In shallow waters along all the coasts of the world, there is an epifauna of sea weeds – green, brown, or red algae. These are the primary producers upon which all the consumers ultimately depend. Of them, brown algae (*Laminaria*) form the majority. Not only does *Laminaria* provide food but, at low tide, it protects the animals beneath it from desiccation and sunlight. Moreover, the surfaces of its fronds are often encrusted by moss animals (polyzoans) and cnidarian polyps. (Cnidaria is a phylum of primitive animals that includes sea anemones, jellyfish, corals and their allies.) These are preyed upon by sea slugs (nudibranchs) some of which feed exclusively on polyzoans, others on hydroid polyps. Not only sea weeds but also eel grasses (*Zostera*) and other higher plants grow in shallow sea water, providing food for many marine animals including turtles.

Deep waters

Deeper waters extend from the edges of the continental shelf to the deepest ocean trenches. They comprise the **benthic zone**. The organisms that inhabit this zone are frequently stalked and anchored above the muddy ooze or sediment that covers the sea bed. This ooze is composed largely of the shells of foraminiferidans, which are calcareous. Indeed, chalk is made up almost entirely of the shells of Foraminiferida that died many millions of years ago. Other important constituents of ooze are radiolarians and diatoms, both of which have siliceous shells.

Calcareus skeletons usually predominate in the tropical and warm temperate regions. They can be subdivided into **globigerina ooze** (named after the most plentiful type of foraminiferidan), **coccolith ooze** (formed from the calcareous plates of coccolithopores) and **pteropod ooze**. Pteropods are small swimming marine snails. Calcareous ooze covers an area of about 128 million km^2. **Diatomaceous** and **radiolarian oozes** (formed from the shells of siliceous microorganisms) occupy some 38 million km^2, especially on the bottom of temperate and polar seas; while a further 102 million km^2 is covered with inorganic red clay.

The number of animal species that inhabit the abyss is relatively small. Many of these species are cosmopolitan and can be divided into two groups – mud eaters and predators. Among the first are starfish, brittle stars and polychaete worms. The second includes crustaceans and fishes.

Hydrothermal vents

At one time it was believed that the ultimate source of energy for life on Earth came only through photosynthesis, as described in Chapter 2. It is, however, now known that some food chains are based not on sunlight but on chemosynthetic energy. The best known example is the extraordinary ecosystem of tube-worms, clams and other animals that live on the deep ocean floor close to volcanic **hydrothermal** vents. No sunlight reaches such depths and at the base of all these food chains are bacteria that grow by using the chemical energy of the reaction between atmospheric oxygen dissolved in the sea water and sulphide in the hydrothermal fluids issuing from the vents. These specialised bacteria grow inside the tissues of some of the more highly adapted vent animals which have no mouths or intestines but exist by assimilating metabolites produced by the bacteria. There are many other examples of bacterial communities that are dependent on chemical energy derived from gases or liquids coming from the earth, but none support food chains as do those of hydrothermal vents. Indeed, it is by no means impossible (although it is unlikely) that life may have evolved in such situations.

Geothermal areas are widespread, although restricted to special locations throughout the world. The microorganisms that live around hydrothermal vents are **thermophilic** and thrive at high temperatures. Most thermophiles are capable of growth at 55 to 60 °C but a few archaebacteria can survive at around 90 °C. Most of them are restricted to a limited range of temperatures, so the distances of various species from the submarine vents themselves are critical. Hydrostatic pressure increases the boiling point of water and, owing to the low solubility of oxygen at high temperatures, there is a tendency for extreme thermophiles to be anaerobic and metabolise without using oxygen.

Rocky shores

Rocky shores are the typical habitat of epiflora and epifauna. They form part of the **littoral zone**, the region between low- and high-tide marks. The extent of this zone is governed by variations in tidal range from **spring tides**, shortly after full and new moons, and **neap tides**, a week later when the range between maximum and minimum levels is much less than in spring tides. The local configuration of the coastline can also have a profound effect. On the Atlantic coast of the USA the range is less than a metre while in the inner part of the Bay of Fundy between New Brunswick and Nova Scotia it is as much as 15 m. In the Baltic and Mediterranean, which are almost completely landlocked, the tidal range is only about 30 to 50 cm.

The fury of the waves breaking against the land and washing away loose stones and pebbles creates a typical rocky shore. This is a harsh environment for plants and animals as they are exposed to extremes of temperature, dry air or sea water, light or darkness. In rock pools they lead a more sheltered existence but, when rain falls, the water may become brackish. Here one can find green seaweeds, forests of calcareous, coralline sea weeds or nullipores, sea anemones, topshells, barnacles, prawns, crabs, shore fishes and many other plants and animals.

Perhaps the most striking feature of rocky shores is the **zonation** of both plants and animals. This depends upon the varying extent to which different species can withstand exposure to the air when the tide is low. It is also affected by latitude because the heat and sunlight are stronger nearer to the equator. In Britain the dominant plants near the low tide mark are the bladder wrack (*Fucus serratus*) and various oar weeds such as *Laminaria digitata*. At higher levels are zones dominated by other species of sea weed, each with its characteristic fauna. Particularly well studied animals on British shores are periwinkles (*Littorina*) which extend over the various zones of seaweeds from *L. littorea* at the lowest levels to *L. neritoides* which exists in the splash zone well above high-tide mark (Figure 5.3). A comparable example is afforded by the zonation of barnacles.

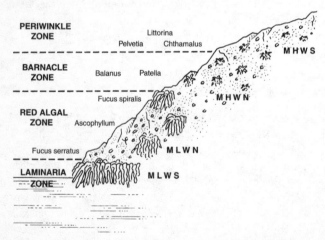

5.3 Typical north European barnacle-dominated zonation on rocky shores. MHWS = Mean high water spring tide level; MHWN = Mean high water neap tide level; MLWN = Mean low water neap tide level; MLWS = Mean low water spring tide level.

Sandy and muddy shores

In some places, the action of powerful cross currents deposits banks of sand formed by the abrasion of rocks while, at the mouths of rivers, there are mud flats composed of sediment washed down from the land. The vertical distribution of animals in sand and mud is far more obscure than that on rocks, and the zonation of the different species is less clear.

Three different strata of animals are usually found:

1 Surface-dwelling crustaceans and polychaetes (such as the ragworm *Nereis*) which burrow actively;

2 A region of bivalve molluscs – cockles, razor shells, clams and so on;

3 A deeper zone of burrowing polychaete worms, such as the lugworm (*Arenicola marina*) whose ubiquitous presence is revealed by the numerous worm casts which form a characteristic feature of muddy shores.

Coral reefs and mangrove swamps

Oceanic islands burst from the sea as sterile volcanic cones, usually associated with the submarine ridges that run down the centres of the Atlantic and Indian Oceans and in a complex lattice-work across the Pacific. In tropical regions their coastlines are usually fringed with coral. If the island subsides or the water rises the coral, which cannot live at a depth below about 40 m, grows upward in an ever-widening reef until it forms an atoll. Coral reefs also fringe the borders of the continents in many tropical regions. They are the marine equivalent of tropical rainforest and are of two kinds: **fringing reefs** near to the land and **barrier reefs** separated from the shore by a wide, deep channel. They owe their existence to the skeletons of millions of tiny colonial cnidarian polyps of various kinds and develop over long periods of time.

Coral reefs have the most abundant fauna of any natural ecosystem. Reef development requires the water to be at least 20 °C and with a salinity similar to that of the open sea. Consequently reefs are restricted to regions between latitudes 30°N and 30°S and are not found near the mouths of large rivers such as the Amazon or Congo. Such places are usually occupied by mangrove swamps (see below). The reef flora includes a number of seaweed species, calcareous algae and sea grasses, but by far the most important are unicellular **dinoflagellates**. They are present in billions within the inner layer of the coral polyps' tissues and both they and the polyps obtain mutual benefit from the association, as we shall see in Chapter 10. The dinoflagellates enable or induce the coral polyps to deposit much greater quantities of skeleton than do corals that lack them.

Reefs of living coral are breathtakingly beautiful. The corals themselves are highly coloured, many being deep brown with violet, pink or white polyps. Others are green or yellow and the other animals present are coloured equally vividly. Innumerable fishes of varied and striking hues dash in shoals among the forests of coral and there are many colourful tube worms with brilliant crowns of tentacles, large anemones, sea cucumbers, molluscs and innumerable crabs and other crustaceans living in association with the coral. In addition, the shells of the molluscs and crustaceans are often encrusted with sponges, sea mats and other sedentary animals, themselves extremely colourful.

Estuaries form a special ecosystem in the littoral zone and in the tropics – Central and South America, Africa, Malaysia and Indonesia – usually develop into steamy mangrove swamps. These mud flats are traversed by canals and support a dense growth of mangrove trees with stilt-like roots. The dominant species is *Rhizophora manga*, but a variety of plants with a similar growth habit are also found. Because of their abundant leaves, the surface of the mud is protected from the tropical sun. Between and upon the roots creep millions of tiny crabs whose coloration usually matches that of the mangrove bark. Fiddler crabs (*Uca*) wave their brightly coloured claws from the entrances to their burrows and hermit crabs scuttle among mangrove roots encrusted with various types of sea oysters. Mud skippers (*Periopthalmus*) live more out of water than in it. These small fishes feed on small insects as well as on tiny crabs.

Fresh waters

Fresh water rivers, lakes and inland seas comprise innumerable bodies of water, varying in size and depth and spread across the continents of the world. Compared with the sea, even the deepest of inland waters are shallow. Only Lake Baikal (1706 m) and Lake Nyasa (1435 m) are deeper than 1000 m whereas the average figure for the oceans is about 3795 m.

Lakes and pools grade into marshes and a similar gradation is found in running waters. Consequently, the extent of the shore and shallow bottom is, relatively, very much greater in inland waters than it is in the sea.

The most important physical and climatic factors other than light in aquatic environments – often referred to as **hydroclimates** – include the following:

1 **Density**. Water is nearly one thousand times heavier than air and its density increases with depth and salinity. The density of protoplasm is slightly greater than that of sea water so the tendency for living organisms to sink is even greater in freshwater;

2 **Pressure**. As in the ocean, the pressure of water at great depths is enormous, but since it permeates the bodies of living organisms it has no appreciable effect;

3 **Salinity**. The salt content of the open sea is relatively uniform, but that of fresh waters may vary by a factor of more than 20. Salinity affects aquatic plants and animals, not so much through its influence on the density of the water as by the **osmotic pressure** that it exerts. (**Osmosis** is the diffusion of a solvent through a partially permeable membrane into a more concentrated solution on the other side of the membrane. Solutions with high osmotic pressures tend to absorb moisture from living organisms, while those with low osmotic pressures cause their tissues to become waterlogged and over diluted);

4 **Acidity**. This may have a considerable influence on the flora and fauna of fresh waters. The waters of bog lakes are usually acid, dark coloured and sparsely populated. In contrast, the high concentration of alkaline carbonates and a low content of carbon dioxide, characteristic of many hill streams, constitute a more favourable environment for plants and animals;

5 **Temperature**. Like other climatic factors, temperature tends to be more uniform in aquatic than in terrestrial environments. This is because the **specific heat** of water is about 500 times greater than that of air, and the thermal conductivity is approximately 20 times greater. The most profound effects of temperature are concerned with the stratification of the water.

Thermal stratification

Warm water is less dense than cold and consequently floats to the surface of a lake. This leads to temperature layering or stratification. Water is most dense around 4 °C when it sinks to the bottom, displacing to the surface water that is even colder. Further cooling may lead to the formation of ice. But for this change in density at 4 °C, there would be a tendency for lakes to freeze solid in winter. The lakes of temperate latitudes become thermally stratified most often during the period of summer stagnation. This overturns in late autumn when water cooler than 4 °C moves from the depths and, again, in spring when warmer water floats upward and the colder water sinks.

The surface waters of lakes are known as the **epilimnion** (Figure 5.4). Stirred by the wind, with plenty of light and oxygen, they support a rich

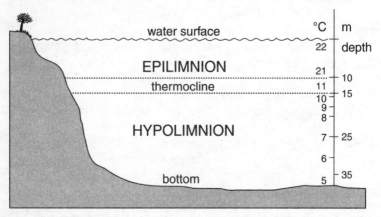

5.4 Stratification in a temperate climate lake in summer.

floating flora and fauna. The phytoplankton consists of bacteria, microscopic diatoms and cyanobacteria and provides abundant food for the zooplankton. This is composed of protozoans (animal-like Protista), wheel-animalcules or rotifers, water fleas (*Daphnia*), insect larvae and so on (Figure 5.5). Many planktonic species are cosmopolitan and can be found throughout the world. Their adaptations for floating include a large surface to volume ratio often enhanced by the possession of numerous spines which reduce the rate of sinking, gelatinous tissue (Figure 5.5(a)) and floats which lower specific gravity.

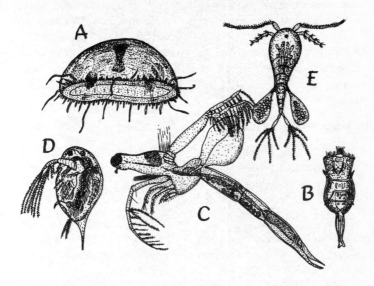

5.5 Freshwater zooplanktonic animals: (a) Jellyfish (b) Rotifer; (c) *Leptodora*; (d) *Daphnia*; (e) *Cyclops*. (The last three are all Crustacea.)

Anybody with a modicum of zoological training should be able to see at a glance that the animal illustrated in Figure 5.5(c) (*Leptodora*) is a predatory planktonic crustacean. The numerous hairs and spines indicate that it is planktonic. Its large eyes and **raptory** forelimbs which snatch at its prey show how it feeds, while its arthropodan characters are unmistakably crustacean, including the oar-like antennae with which it swims.

The epilimnion extends to a depth of 10 m or so. Below it is a transitional area or **thermocline** in which the temperature shows maximum rates of change with depth. The deepest water, or **hypolimnion**, seldom experiences an annual thermal range in excess of 5 °C. There is no light there and oxygen may be deficient; so plants are absent and animals scarce.

Deep tropical lakes such as Nyasa, Kivu and Atitlán in Guatemala – in which the water never circulates – are said to be **meromictic**. The lower levels are anaerobic; carbon dioxide, methane and hydrogen sulphide are produced and only tubifex worms, midge larvae and so on are able to inhabit them.

Lakes that circulate twice yearly, in spring and autumn, are called **dimictic**. They are characteristic of temperate regions. **Monomictic** lakes circulate once per annum, while **oligomictic** lakes circulate only at rare intervals when abnormal cold spells prevail. They are restricted to tropical and subtropical regions, but **polymictic** lakes – which show no persistent thermal stratification at any time because they are large and shallow – are found in all parts of the world.

Vertical migration

Increasing depth of water is characterised by decreasing light intensity. This is the driving factor behind the diurnal vertical migration of the plankton as it is in the pelagic zone of the oceans. These migrations are extremely well documented both in marine plankton and also in the plankton of inland waters.

In Lake Windermere, for instance, the copepod crustacean *Cyclops strenuus* is at its greatest abundance at some depth from the surface in late morning. As the day draws on, there is an upward migration and, around midnight, the surface waters of the lake are most densely populated. There is a strong correlation between the depth of penetration of the blue segment of the light spectrum and the position of greatest abundance of *C. strenuus*. Moreover, the copepods move to greater depths in summer, when the light intensity is greatest, than they do in spring.

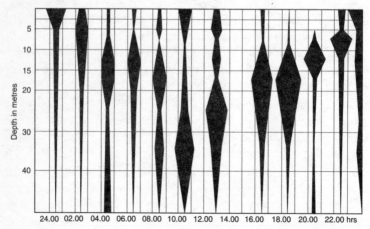

5.6 Daily migration of *Cyclops* in Lake Windermere (after P. Ullyott).

Similar migrations have been described in *Daphnia* and other zooplankton. They may enable these consumers to remain among the phytoplankton on which they feed. Nevertheless they are physiologically a direct innate response to light intensity and time of day. The consumers are not merely following the movements of the producers on which they feed.

In the present section the conditions that obtain in larger fresh water lakes have been indicated. In streams and rivers the speed of current and corresponding nature of the bottom are the factors that probably affect the flora and fauna most. Types of streams and the plants and animals inhabiting them have been analysed by many authors (*see* Bibliography).

The multiplicity of environmental conditions in inland water and the varied combinations of light, temperature, chemical content and so on, result in a wealth of species that are very different from those in the oceans. There are many more marine than fresh water phyla. The number of types may be limited in inland waters but, within any individual genus, there is almost unlimited variation.

6 | POPULATIONS AND THEIR REGULATION

In Chapters 4 and 5, analyses have been made of the climatic and edaphic factors that determine the flora and fauna of the world's various biomes. In this chapter, we begin to consider the ecology of organisms that occupy the same ecosystems and which, therefore, interact among themselves. These interactions may be autecological within the same species, or synecological involving several species. Let us first consider those factors that regulate the sizes of populations of the same species.

Population growth and its limitations

People tend to speak somewhat glibly of the balance of nature, as though this not only existed but was properly understood. In fact, the agencies that regulate the numbers of plants and animals, and their modes of operation in nature, are still among the most complicated and least well understood aspects of ecology. Of course, we know the extremes. When food runs out, a population that depends upon it also dies out: but the situation is seldom as simple as this under natural conditions. When food is present in excess, populations increase up to a certain point, but no more. Even the most slowly reproducing species would soon cover the world if its population growth were not restricted. In his *Essay on the Principle of Population as it affects the future improvement of Society*, R.T. Malthus (1798) explained that this implied 'a strong and constantly operating check' on population growth. The ideas of Malthus undoubtedly influenced Charles Darwin in summarising his own views *On the Origin of Species* (1859).

During the period of rapid development in ecological investigations that took place at the beginning of the twentieth century, Raymond Pearl in America was among the first to apply statistical methods to population data. Although the study of populations is essentially quantitative, I shall not go into the complicated mathematics involved. Even under the most favourable conditions, the populations of all living organisms tend to rise slowly at first. This is merely because individuals are scarce and seldom meet. The rate steadily increases exponentially, however, in proportion to the numbers present, until, as a result of various factors to be discussed, it reaches a state of equilibrium or, more dramatically, there is a crash in numbers. Thus the increase in population plotted against time usually shows a **sigmoid** or **S-shaped** logistic curve in which, not surprisingly, there are numerous small irregularities. When the increase culminates not in levelling off but in a precipitous decline in numbers, the growth curve is referred to as being **J-shaped**.

Pearl demonstrated logistic growth in laboratory populations of yeast cells and fruit flies (*Drosophila melanogaster*), G.F. Gause in *Paramecium caudatum* and Thomas Park in the flour beetle *Tribolium confusum*. Many other workers have obtained similar results with different organisms. Every population eventually reaches a theoretical maximum or **asymptote** (carrying capacity of its environment), which is determined by the circumstances peculiar to that particular population (Figure 6.1). Mathematicians are still calculating and recalculating the asymptote for the human population of the world. But this assumes that the curve will be S-shaped. Let us hope that it does not turn out to be J-shaped!

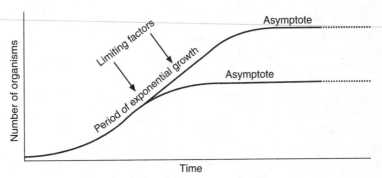

6.1   Sigmoid or logistic population growth curve showing two possible asymptotes at different levels according to circumstances.

A big problem for population ecologists is to ascertain what factors determine the levels of the asymptotes of the populations they are studying. The first, most obvious environmental factor is shortage of food.

If Figure 6.1 were taken to represent the numbers of zooplankton feeding upon phytoplankton in an aquarium, the higher of the two asymptotes might be approached if the plant nutrients in the culture were to be increased. It is difficult to maintain laboratory populations at a steady asymptotic level without much variability for long, but this has been achieved in the case of yeast cells over periods of about six weeks. When microorganisms are studied in cultures, population numbers are usually based on sample counts.

Even in the presence of ample food, however, populations eventually cease to increase. In the case of *Tribolium confusum*, this has been shown to be due to **conditioning** of the flour in which the beetles live. By conditioning we mean altering the physical and/or chemical quality of the environment. As populations of flour beetles never leave their flour, they will inevitably condition it after a while – mainly by adding contaminants such as faecal pellets, moulted integuments and dead bodies. If this conditioned flour is sieved off and replaced by fresh flour, a new and higher asymptote is soon reached. It has been shown that heavily conditioned flour, in which large cultures have lived, induces population decline mainly through a reduction in the **fecundity** of the surviving beetles and an increase in the length of larval development. Fecundity means the rate at which eggs are laid and the total number produced, whether they are fertile or not. It has also been found that even slightly conditioned flour reduces egg production significantly. Conditioning appears to reduce fecundity through its effect on males as well as on females. If the flour is not renewed, larval and pupal mortality also increase.

Even in the absence of food shortage and conditioning, populations of living organisms eventually reach their natural asymptotic levels. As they grow even more numerous, **density** itself becomes a regulating factor. When male flour beetles compete for females in crowded conditions, they often jostle each other at the critical moment of mating so that, in the end, fewer females are fertilised than would have been the case had fewer males initially been present. Secondly, flour beetles are rather indiscriminate feeders and occasionally eat their own eggs by mistake. The denser the population, the higher will be the ratio of eggs to flour grains and the greater will be the proportion of eggs eaten.

The effects of high density are manifold and vary in different species. Conditioning of a medium by one species does not, however, necessarily confer adverse effects upon another species living in the same medium.

Moreover, many animals – both experimentally and in their natural surroundings – reproduce more quickly when there is a certain degree of crowding. Additionally, some do not breed at all when their populations are greatly reduced. This is a big problem for conservationists.

Many criticisms have been levelled against the concept of the logistic curve. Nevertheless, when not overinterpreted but used merely as an empirical record of population growth, it is undoubtedly a valuable demographic tool – as emphasised by W.C. Allee and his co-authors as long ago as 1949 in their monumental *Principles of Animal Ecology*.

Intraspecific and interspecific predation under experimental conditions

The egg cannibalism under crowded conditions demonstrated experimentally in *Tribolium confusum* is an example of the well-known fact that the more crowded predatory animals are, the greater the amount of killing and cannibalism that is sure to take place. Interspecific competition is a problem of much greater complexity than cannibalism and also one of much greater ecological significance. Predation of one species on another ranges from situations that are relatively simple to others that are extremely complex.

An illustration of predation among laboratory populations is provided by the work of Gause in the 1930s. In this, cultures of bacteria formed the base of a food chain exploited by the ciliate *Paramecium caudatum*. The latter, in turn, was eaten by a secondary consumer, another ciliate named *Didinium nasutum*. Gause's interest lay in seeing whether he could reproduce in the laboratory the theoretical oscillations (previously predicted by A.J. Lotka and V. Volterra) between predator and prey (Figure 6.2a). In some experiments, the predators (*Didinium*) ate all the prey (*Paramecium*) and then died out themselves (Figure 6.2b). When the environment was rendered less homogeneous by introducing 'refuges', different end results were obtained. (The refuges consisted of cloudy patches of dilute porridge in which the *Paramecium* could hide.) Under these circumstances the predators exploited their prey in the clear portions of the medium. At first they multiplied slightly but then starved while those prey that had escaped capture, because they were in the refuges, then increased in numbers (Figure 6.2c). Finally, when both species were introduced into a clear medium with

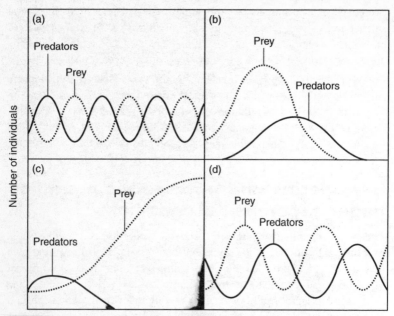

6.2 Predator–prey interactions between protozoan populations: (a) Theoretical balanced oscillations; (b) Prey all consumed and predators starve; (c) With a 'refuge' present some prey escape but nevertheless all predators starve; (d) Oscillation achieved by means of new introductions (based on the work of G.F. Gause).

subsequent reintroductions, it was possible to obtain a few **cycles** of growth of the prey population (Figure 6.2d).

Results of this kind which have subsequently been obtained with many other species of Protista and animals, are probably limited almost entirely to experimental populations. In nature, sufficient numbers of the prey normally escape for extinction to be avoided. When they become somewhat scarce, the predators switch to another source of food. Changes in the diet of mammalian predators such as lions or leopards are the normal response to temporary shortages of their customary prey. Even cheetahs – whose normal prey consists of Thomson's gazelles which they are highly specialised to catch – will capture wildebeest calves when gazelles are in short supply.

Density dependent and density independent controls

During the 1950s there was considerable disagreement among ecologists as to the ways in which the various forces operate that tend to maintain short term stable inter-relationships between populations and to regulate their densities. Intra-specific competition may take place for territory, shelter and food when these are in short supply, thus reducing the birth rate. Different species that have similar requirements may also compete with one another unless migration takes place. The situation is made infinitely more complicated, however, by the effects of predation, parasites and disease. It was in the relative degrees of importance of the various types of factors controlling a population that the disagreement chiefly lay.

Some ecologists thought that the agents which determine population densities in nature must be of two kinds, **density independent** and **density dependent**. The former were defined as bearing equally heavily upon a population whether its density was great or small: undoubtedly the most drastic of these would be climatic – such as frost, drought or floods. But, it was agreed, in order to regulate the density of a population within definite limits, the factors responsible would have to be able to destroy a greater proportion when the density of the population was high than when it was low. Of the density dependent mortality factors which play most heavily upon a population when it has reached a maximum number, the most important are competition between individuals for shelter and food, predators, parasites, disease and the effects of migration.

Let us, for example, consider predation as a density dependent factor regulating the size of a population of herbivores. First, an individual predator usually captures and eats more prey per unit time as the prey density increases – until some point of satiation is reached. Above this, the rate of consumption is constant. Second, the number of predators usually increases if an increased number of prey is available for sufficiently long. For instance, the number of foxes and snowy owls feeding on lemmings in the Arctic increases or decreases as the size of the lemming population changes. The two kinds of response may occur separately or simultaneously and can interact with one another. Invertebrate predators control the population size of their prey only by increasing in numbers, but they can do so very rapidly. Vertebrate predators, in contrast, can switch their diet from one type of prey to another which has become more readily available. Rapid reproduction is not, therefore, essential for them to be able to control the numbers of prey.

However, some biologists (notably H.G. Andrewartha and L.C. Birch in 1954) argued that it was not necessary to invoke the concept of density dependent factors since natural control was achieved chiefly by climatic factors. Examples were cited, especially from among insects, whose numbers seem to spend most of the time recovering by annual increases from periodic climatic setbacks.

No doubt the truth lies somewhere between the two extremes and both types of control take place to varying degrees among different species and in different ecosystems. Insecticides operate in a density independent manner but, when a gardener sprays only the infested leaves of a rose bush, the insecticide is being applied in a density dependent way. At any rate, the argument that density independent factors alone theoretically cannot control population numbers has completely died away. Possibly climate may control the numbers of a species for much of the time, while density dependent factors are significantly invoked only when maximum or minimum densities are reached. In any case, no one will disagree with the statement that population sizes are directly controlled by environmental influences of one sort or another. If these are sufficiently complex, no one species can become too numerous: but where they are simpler, it is easier for plague proportions to be reached.

In recent years it has been shown that even simple and deterministic first-order difference equations – concerned, for instance, with the relative numbers of a single predator and a single prey species – can exhibit a surprising array of dynamic behaviour. This includes stable points, a bifurcating hierarchy of stable cycles, and apparently random fluctuations which negate the various assumptions upon which the earlier arguments had been based. These can only be interpreted in terms of the chaos theory.

The potential birth rates of all animal species are extremely high. Even the slowest breeders, such as elephants, would soon reach fantastic numbers if a large proportion were not killed off in some way or another long before death from old age, which must be a rare occurrence, intervened. The statement is sometimes made that, if all were to survive, the progeny of a single pair of aphids would, within a season, produce a heap of insects as high as Mount Everest. This is really quite meaningless, however, because from an ecological point of view the animal does not exist independently of its environment. Not only do innumerable aphids fall victim to various predators and parasites but, even if this were not so, food shortage would impose a check to further increase in numbers long before there were enough to build even a small molehill. Arctic animals, such as snowshoe rabbits and lemmings, show marked cycles in numbers. At the upper limits of these, however, mass emigrations occur.

On the whole the activities of human beings create simpler conditions than would normally occur in nature. The growing of crops, the herding of animals, bulk storage, urbanisation – all these result in a relative lack of natural checks to sudden population increases. For economic reasons humans destroy complexity and replace it by large tracts of uniformity. Consequently conditions conducive to plagues of one form or another are inevitably created.

As long ago as 1907, E.Ray Lankester wrote:

But it is not only by his reckless mixing up of incompatibles from all parts of the globe that the unscientific man has risked the conversion of paradise into a desert. In his greedy efforts to produce large quantities of animals and plants convenient for his purposes, and in his eagerness to mass and organize his own race for defence and conquest, man has accumulated unnatural crowds of his own kind in towns and fortresses. Such undiluted masses of one organism serve as a ready field for the propagation of previously rare and unimportant parasites from individual to individual.

Although by no means well established, various lines of evidence, derived primarily from population studies of dominant or abundant species, suggest that density dependent processes also have an impact on natural plant populations. Experimental monocultures of annuals, such as crimson clover (*Trifolium incarnatum*) and Italian rye grass (*Lolium perenne multiflorum*), have shown that, with increasing density, the inequality between the sizes of plants within the cultures increases also. Survival, growth and reproduction of the perennial bunch grass (*Bouteloua rigidiseta*) in Texas has been shown to be greatly dependent upon the size of the plants. At higher densities, average size decreases.

Effects of parasites

When a population remains relatively constant and the point or line about which it oscillates is moderately stationary, its powers of increase or **biotic potential** must approximately equal **environmental resistance**. This is a combination of density dependent and density independent control factors. The history of economic entomology is replete with the records of unintentional 'experiments' in which organisms have been taken to new environments which contained little or no environmental resistance in the form of suitable predators, parasites or competitors. In many cases, physical conditions were similar to those in the original environment, but the lack of biotic resistance allowed the biotic potential of the species to express itself and populations to rise to unprecedented numbers.

When the sugar cane leaf hopper (*Perkinsiella saccharicida*) was introduced into the Hawaiian Islands, for example, its rate of reproduction was unimpeded. Parasites were later introduced and the leaf hopper population reduced to a level that was no longer of economic importance. This is the principle of **biological control**, which is essentially density dependent. **Chemical control**, by means of insecticides, has sometimes been regarded as being density independent and, therefore, ultimately incapable of controlling pests because the same proportion of the pest population is killed whether the latter is sparse or dense. The use of insecticides is not truly density independent, however, and they do control insect pests as everyone knows. This may be because their application is density dependent and, therefore, according to the argument summarised above, enables their use successfully to control the populations of pests. The modern approach to pest control consists of combining chemical with numerous different types of biological control.

In a fascinating book, *The Ecology of Invasions by Animals and Plants* (1958), Charles Elton, pioneer of animal ecology, discussed numerous examples of population explosions that have occurred in comparatively recent times due to human agencies. These have occurred among infectious pathogens such as the influenza virus, in bacteria like those responsible for bubonic plague, fungi like that of the potato disease, green plants such as the prickly pear, or insects and mammals including rabbits and grey squirrels.

Parasitism

One of the most universal density dependent types of reaction between one species and another is that which finds expression in the phenomenon of **parasitism**. It is almost impossible to give a concise explanation of what biologists understand by the term parasite. Literally, the word means 'one which eats beside another' and parasitism is the interaction between parasites and their hosts. We have already encountered parasitic plants in our discussion of the flora of the tropical rainforest (Chapter 4). Whereas a predatory animal kills its host, living on the capital of its food resource, a parasite lives on the income. It usually does some harm to its host, however, and in extreme cases may cause its death. The parasite depends upon the host for part or all of its life history and the consequences of this dependence may have considerable biological significance since both host and parasite become more or less adapted to one another as a result of their association.

Parasites may induce considerable physiological and morphological changes in their hosts, for example by upsetting the hormones that regulate development, or by interfering with the reproduction glands thereby causing **parasitic castration** and the production of sterile intersexes and thus reducing the biotic potential of the host. A classical example of this is afforded by the bizarre crustacean *Sacculina carcini* which is parasitic upon the shore crab (*Carcinus maenas*). Although related to the barnacle, in its adult state *Sacculina* is little more than a sac containing reproductive organs attached to the abdomen of its host by a mass of root-like tubules that ramify through the crab's tissues. As a result of parasitism, male crabs develop female characteristics, while female crabs regress to a juvenile state. The crustacean affinities of *Sacculina* were only appreciated when it was found to have a special kind of larva, the **nauplius**, which is characteristic of Crustacea.

Most pathogenic **microparasites** (e.g. viruses, bacteria and fungi) have direct reproduction within the host whereas the majority of **macroparasites** (e.g. nematode and platyhelminth worms, annelids and arthropods) have no direct reproduction within one host. Many of the parasites of vertebrates are transmitted through the bites of insects in which parts of their life cycles are passed. Parasites are important contributors to many ecological interactions and in some cases are a major mortality factor. In some cases parasites may cause the death of their hosts directly –

parasitic infections are a primary factor causing infant mortality in developing countries. In others, they may weaken their hosts so that they are rendered vulnerable to predators.

As a matter of convenience, parasites can be roughly divided into external, or **ectoparasites** (e.g. leeches, lice and ticks) and internal, or **endoparasites** (e.g. malarial parasites, roundworms and tapeworms) but this is not always helpful as innumerable intermediate stages exist. Furthermore, the attentions of ectoparasites may cause reactions in the internal organs of their hosts. So, when the interactions of the two are considered, the distinction between external and internal parasites tends to lose its significance.

Before considering predators, the other major group of secondary and tertiary consumers, mention should be made of **parasitoids**. These are the larvae of insects such as ichneumons and tachinid flies which begin their lives as parasites of other insects or spiders. Later they develop into internal carnivores and kill their host. When true parasites become well adapted to their hosts both exhibit considerable **tolerance**: it is usually disadvantageous for a parasite to kill its host. Parasitoids, which combine the characteristics of both parasites and predators, are very important density dependent factors controlling many insect populations and have been much used in the biological control of pests.

Multiparasitism, the simultaneous infestation of the same individual host by two or more species of primary parasitoid, may cause the death of one or both parasitoids. For example, the ichneumon *Compopler* dies when the tachinid *Ernestia rudis* is present but another tachinid, *Therion*, itself has little chance of survival since it is the slowest to attain the destructive feeding stage. **Superparasitism** is the name given to that phase of multiparasitism in which two or more parasites of the same species occur in the same host. Finally, **hyperparasitism** occurs when the primary parasite is attacked by its own specific parasitoid. It seems probable that hyperparasitism is a development of multiparasitism and it is indeed sometimes difficult to distinguish the two. Outside the Hymenoptera examples are rare, but the phenomenon occurs in some bee-flies (Bombyliidae) (*see* Chapter 10 for further information).

Effects of predators

Perhaps the simplest way in which two members of the same species come into density dependent conflict is when one preys upon the other. Animal populations are largely regulated by their death rate: perpetuation of the species takes precedence over survival of the individual. As Tennyson aptly wrote of nature: 'So careful of the type she seems, so careless of the single life'. It is not surprising therefore that, through the ages, carnivorous and omnivorous animals should have evolved behaviour patterns that tend to offset the loss by death of the proteins and other compounds concentrated in their species. For instance, several species of birds, including gulls and owls, are known to eat their own eggs or doomed offspring when food is critically short. As already mentioned, egg cannibalism among flour beetles increases with increasing density and can have an important influence on population dynamics. It is not clear, however, whether cannibalism is always density dependent, or whether it generally stabilises or destabilises populations. Unlike predation, cannibalism usually represents more than just the acquisition of food resources and no general theory predicting its distribution, forms and consequences has yet been formulated. (Predation will be discussed further in Chapter 10.)

In many ways host–parasite and predator–prey relationships are similar. Parasites and predators benefit while host and prey are adversely affected to a greater or lesser degree. The experimental studies of G.F. Gause using *Didinium nasutum* and *Paramecium caudatum* have already been described. In nature, only a few populations actually undergo regular oscillations. Lemmings, voles and snowy owls, for instance, show a three to five year oscillation, ptarmigans, muskrats, snowshoe rabbits and lynxes, one of nine to ten years. These are, however, Arctic animals and the regularity of their population cycles may well be due to the fact that the basic predator–prey oscillation in an ecologically simple biome such as tundra is little disturbed by other factors. In contrast, the equatorial rainforest, because of its extreme complexity, has the greatest inherent stability of any biogeographical region. A tremendous richness of species tends to give a buffering effect to any unusual population change.

r-K selection

The strength at which regulating factors play on the different age groups of a species depends upon the rate of growth of the population. In temperate and Arctic biomes where populations tend to be reduced by catastrophic density independent environmental factors, they recover by increased fecundity and a rapid growth rate (r). In the more constant environment of the humid tropics, populations remain near the limit imposed by resources (K). Varying positions can be allocated to different species along an **r-K spectrum**.

In deserts, for example, long-lived scorpions (Figure 3.4) and tenebrionid beetles are K-selected whereas camel-spiders (Solifugae) (Figure 3.3), and flies – which never have less than one generation during the year and usually many more – are said to be r-selected. In general, K-selected species tend to be larger, to have fewer offspring, longer development and to show a greater degree of parental care than do comparable r-selected species. The concept of r-K selection has been much discussed and criticised. Nevertheless, it occupies an important place in current ecological thought.

Migration

At the peaks of their population oscillations, many species of animal respond to the competition by moving to 'pastures new.' The movement of animals such as lemmings, crossbills and waxwings from their home territory at times of overcrowding are known as **emigration**. In this way population pressure is reduced and numbers regulated. There are three basic types of animal movement: **trivial**, **nomadic** and **migratory**. Trivial movement is found mainly among lower animals of sedentary habit. Thus the common limpet may, when browsing on the seashore, wander as much as a metre from its scar on the rock face. But it never fails to return to its 'home' when the tide recedes because its shell has grown to fit a particular area of the rock surface.

Nomadism is the practice of leading a wandering life and is based on the need to find food. It is characterised by the regularity of the movements involved. This is particularly apparent in the case of animals such as moose which make a restricted area their home for part of the year and are only truly nomadic at other times. In winter, moose collect together and retire to some sheltered area where they remain until the spring returns.

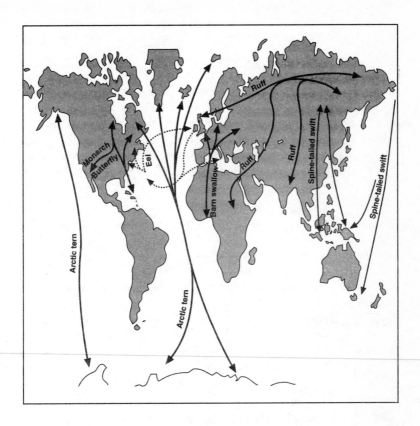

6.3 A selection of routes followed by some outstanding migrants over land and sea.

During the warmer seasons, moose are nomadic over a vast expanse of country.

The third type of animal movement, migration, is a regular to-and-fro directed movement with a complete cycle. It covers a wide variety of behaviour. Some migratory birds such as Arctic terns and skuas, breed within the Arctic circle and winter south of the equator (Figure 6.3). Other species may move only a few hundred kilometres. The advantage of reproducing in Arctic regions lies in the fact that when the ice melts in spring an abundance of insects is available as food for the nestlings. More bird species breed in the Arctic than in the Antarctic. This is mainly because the land mass of the continents is much greater in the northern than in the southern hemisphere.

Some migrations, like those of swifts and swallows, take place several times within the life of an individual; others are undertaken only once. For instance, the common eel breeds in the Sargasso sea. Its fish-like **leptocephalus** (thin head) larvae are carried to Europe by the Gulf Stream, a journey lasting over two to three years. During this time, the leptocephali grow from less than 6 mm to more than 75 mm in length. On reaching the continental shelf of Europe, an abrupt physical change or **metamorphosis** takes place and a typical cylindrical shape is acquired. The young eels, now known as **elvers**, swim up the rivers in countless numbers. For up to ten or more years they remain in fresh water, feeding and growing. Eventually they become silver in colour, their eyes enlarge and they set out on the return journey to the Sargasso sea, a distance of up to 5600 km (Figure 6.3).

Monarch or milkweed butterflies (*Danaus plexippus*) migrate in vast numbers from their summer homes in the United States and southern Canada to Florida, California and Mexico where they spend the winter in semi-hibernation. Thousands of butterflies may occupy the same tree which, for some unknown reason, is selected by the migrants year after year. As spring approaches the monarchs abandon their winter quarters and begin the long flight back to the regions from which they emigrated the previous year. Here they lay their eggs and die. Two or three generations are passed before the following autumn when the annual southward migration begins again.

Migration may have many functions. Some animals undertake large-scale migrations to reach suitable breeding grounds, others to follow their food or to keep within an equable range of temperature. Some populations exhibit irregular or sporadic movements that are the result of scarcity of food in certain years rather than of seasonal climatic changes. Whatever their cause, emigration and migration play an important role in the maintenance and regulation of animal populations, especially when they operate in a density dependent manner.

The influence of human beings on the numbers of plants and animals is very great. Yet humankind cannot yet control its own population explosion. Nor, as already mentioned, do we know the future shape of our own population curve. When the last of the passenger pigeons died in Cincinnati Zoo on 1 September 1914, the species came to a tragic end. At one time, this North American pigeon had been the most numerous of all birds, flocks of over 2 million individuals having been recorded – which is about ten times the total bird population of the British Isles today. Nevertheless, within a century, the species had been exterminated. At the other end of the scale, within less than 1000 years, if the present increase of humankind were to continue, a mass of people would be standing on each other's shoulders, more than a million deep. By 2000 years, the mountain of humanity, travelling outwards at the speed of light, would have reached the edge of the known universe. This is the human equivalent of the heap of aphids as high as Mount Everest mentioned earlier.

No species exists indefinitely, not even *Homo sapiens*. The resources of the Earth are limited. The environment can never be fully exploited because the organism is an agent of the geological, climatic, seasonal and other changes that take place long before any stable equilibrium has been reached. Whether one regards the future with hope or despair, there cannot be any doubt that the fate of humanity now hangs in the balance.

7 | COMMUNITIES

An ecological community is an assemblage of populations of different species interacting within a particular geographical area. Community structure is affected by energy flow, nutrient cycling, population growth and its regulation, parasitism, predation and competition, as well as by pollination, climate and edaphic factors. Communities vary in size, shape and the interactions of the populations that constitute them. There can be few assemblages of populations of different species in which there are so few interactions that their organisations arise primarily from autecological rather than from synecological processes.

Some ecologists consider that ecological communities are **holistic** and should therefore be studied as entire systems, rather than by examining their component parts. This implies that the totals of their properties are greater than the sums of the individual parts. These totalities are sometimes referred to as **emergent** properties. For instance, a group of trees clustered in a wood has different emergent properties than the same number of trees widely dispersed. The trees that are grouped together shade the ground more, while mounds of rotting leaves tend to accumulate beneath them. This does not occur when trees are spaced widely apart. The holistic concept is not, however, universally accepted. Other ecologists contend that communities are discrete, discontinuous discernable and, therefore, describable entities. They argue that analysis will reveal the fact that populations of certain species reach their optima only in identical communities and would never do so in communities that differed in composition. According to this **organiomic** community view, plant associations are regarded as having objective reality – like an organism or a species – and are therefore capable of being described in a similar way. This altercation is somewhat reminiscent of the dispute over the Gaia hypothesis discussed in Chapter 1.

The places in which various organisms live together in a community are known as habitats, as we saw in Chapter 3. Many species of plant or animal can be found in more than one type of habitat. Moreover, in a pond community, for example, the roots of a water-lily grow at the bottom, while the leaves, floating on the water surface, are in a different habitat (Figure 3.7). The same applies to trees, bushes and most of the larger plants. An extreme example is afforded by the lianas of the tropical forest biome whose stems traverse several different habitats. Animals also are seldom confined to a single habitat but, unlike plants, are able to move from one to another. Some species may occupy two or more habitats which to the human observer appear to have very little in common. For instance, certain rare species of European spiders occur both in heathland and fens; while the lygaeid bug *Ischnodemus sabulei* (Hemiptera Heteroptera) is found not only by the edges of streams and reed swamps but also on the grass *Ammophila arenaria* which grows in sand dunes. It is not known in any other habitat.

Stratification, zonation and dispersion

Not only do different parts of individual plants occupy differing habitats but a casual glance at a plant community shows that the heights of the various components vary. In other words they show stratification. As we have seen in Chapter 4, this is particularly evident in the tropical forest biome (Figure 4.5), especially in areas where the canopy is broken. Where the canopy is intact, it receives much more solar energy than do the layers beneath.

Stratification is apparent not only in the vegetation but also among the animals that inhabit it. Most tropical forest insects fly just above the canopy. In grassland they are mainly to be seen a few centimetres above the herb layer. A second concentration of insects, this time crawling on the soil or burrowing within the litter (L) and humus (Ao) layers, is to be found in both biomes.

Zonation

Stratification is not confined to the land: it is also apparent in aquatic environments. In terrestrial environments, stratification reflects variations in the vegetation. In open waters, on the other hand, both phytoplankton and zooplankton tend to occur in the upper layers, free-swimming fishes below them, then bottom-living crabs, starfish and molluscs and, finally, burrowing worms and crustaceans. On rocky shores, green algae tend to grow nearest to the water surface, brown algae in deeper water and, deeper still, red algae.

Thermal stratification often impedes vertical mixing in aquatic environments. The mixing of deep nutrient-rich and stratified shallow water in the Arctic and Antarctic oceans results in high productivity in the photic zone where photosynthesis takes place. Vertical mixing of water depends upon the input of energy. This energy may be provided by ocean currents, winds and so on. When evaporation exceeds freshwater input, the surface layers of marine systems become more saline and sink below the less dense sea water beneath. Again, when surface water cools in winter, it becomes denser and moves below the less dense underlying layers.

Small lakes in temperate regions are more sensitive to seasonal changes than are the oceans and thermal cycles also shape their nutrient budgets, but to a much lesser extent. The thermocline demarcates an upper epilimnion and a deeper layer of cooler water, the hypolimnion (Figure 5.4). During periods of stratification, bacterial respiration may deplete the amount of oxygen present in the hypolimnion and, if this is prolonged, the water may become anoxic. In the low redox environment of bottom sediment, the reduction of compounds of iron, manganese and nitrate from their oxidised to their reduced forms affects their solubility. This is particularly true of ferric iron (Fe^{3+}) when it is reduced to ferrous iron (Fe^{2+})

Phosphorus is often scarce in the surface layers of lakes, thereby restricting the production of phytoplankton until mixing of the water layers takes place in the autumn and spring. Lakes are often classified in a continuum ranging from poorly nourished (**oligotrophic**) to well nourished (**eutrophic**) lakes. The addition of the nutrients in sewage and water that has drained from artificially fertilised agricultural land may lead to excess eutrophication. This can have adverse effects upon the fish population and render the lake water unsuitable for human consumption.

Dispersion

Within the distribution of a population, the spacing or dispersal of individuals with respect to one another may vary considerably. Indeed, the horizontal spacing or **dispersion** of plants and animals can be used in describing the structure of an ecological community (Figure 7.1). There are three basic types of dispersion:

1 **uniform**
2 **random**
3 **clumped**.

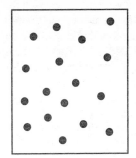 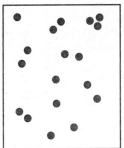 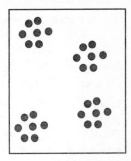

7.1 Basic patterns of dispersal: uniform, random and clumped.

Uniform dispersion, sometimes called **overdispersion**, usually results from competition. Plants situated too close to larger neighbours may suffer from the effects of shading and from root competition for nutrients and water. There may also be competition for pollination, if pollinators are scarce as is often the case in arid regions. Competition for space is reduced when water shortage, rather than light, is the limiting factor (*see* Chapter 2). Competition between desert plants sometimes extends even to the synthesis of **allelopathic** chemicals which inhibit the growth of other plants – both of their own and of other species.

Nearest-neighbour analysis indicates that strong competitive interactions occur between perennial grasses growing on the sides of sand dunes in the Namib and other deserts. These operate both intraspecifically within a vegetation zone and interspecifically where one species replaces another over the dune slopes.

Among animals, the maintenance of a minimum distance between each individual and the nearest neighbour results in even spacing or overdispersal. In their crowded colonies, gulls, gannets and other seabirds place their nests just beyond the reach of their neighbours.

R. Hinde has listed many advantages that accrue to the holders of **territories**. These include exclusive use of resources such as food, reduced predation and disease due to greater spacing from conspecific birds and facilitation of escape from enemies as a result of familiarity with the territorial area. Again, many mammals maintain territories from which potential competitors for food or mates are excluded. Territorial behaviour is also well known among crustaceans, insects, molluscs, fish and reptiles.

Random distribution, in which individuals are distributed throughout a homogeneous area without regard to the presence of others, sometimes occurs – especially among plants – but it must be a somewhat uncommon occurrence in nature except on a relatively small scale. Mathematical measures of dispersal can, however, be compared with the values expected were random dispersion to occur. This random distribution is known as **Poisson** distribution and deviations from it indicate statistically whether dispersal is uniform or clumped (*see* Appendix III).

Clumping or **aggregation** is probably the type of distribution most often encountered in nature. It may result from the uneven distribution of resources such as water and nutrients in the case of plants, or of food sources in the case of animals. Reproductive patterns also may account for clumping. Many organisms show an overall uniform pattern of distribution but one having aggregations within it. A well known example of clumping is displayed every time you overturn a rock or a fallen branch and see masses of woodlice, centipedes, millipedes, springtails (*Collembola*) and other insects, spiders and mites, clustered in the moist atmosphere beneath it. Some of them are there because they require the high humidity, some are vegetarians that feed on rotting vegetation, others are predators that feed on these primary consumers and still others may be sheltering from large predators in the outside world. It is possible to construct an entire food web based on the organisms living beneath a single rotting log.

Patterns of dispersion can change as a function of season or of age. Newborn and juvenile scorpions, for instance, exhibit a strongly clumped pattern, whereas adults are usually either distributed randomly or are overdispersed.

Periodism

Communities are not static; they undergo more or less continued change in their population sizes and in the composition of the species incorporated in them. These changes are dictated by the environment and, indirectly, by the life cycles of the organisms themselves. Each of these has its own characteristic pattern of development. The three principal periodicities to which living organisms are exposed are **diurnal** or **diel**, **lunar** and **tidal** and **seasonal**. The study of the rhythm of the seasons is often referred to as seasonal phenology.

Biological rhythms are of two kinds; **exogenous,** which are no more than responses to the physical changes in the environment over periods of time, and **endogenous**. Endogenous rhythms are driven by the **biological clocks** within living organisms. They persist under constant experimental conditions. Few biologists today doubt that living organisms (other than Monera whose life cycles are usually less than 24 hours) possess biological clocks. Thanks to these, they mirror in their physiology and behaviour the environmental changes that they experience in nature. Most animals probably show **composite** rhythms combining both exogenous and endogenous components. Biological clocks are thought to be self-sustained oscillations whose phases can be reset or **entrained** by an external **synchroniser** or *Zeitgeber* (meaning time giver; a term proposed by J. Aschoff in 1954).

In their natural habitats, the rhythms of most plants and animals are entrained to a frequency of 24 hours by the daily cycles of light and darkness engendered by the rotation of the Earth. Although these diurnal rhythms frequently persist under constant laboratory conditions, their **free-running** periods usually become slightly longer or somewhat shorter than 24 hours. For this reason, F. Halberg coined the word **circadian** (from the Latin *circa*, about, and *dies*, a day) to describe them. Persistent lunar and tidal rhythms are likewise called **circalunadian** (about a lunar day) because the period of the bimodal lunar day rhythm is usually longer or shorter than the period displayed in nature, while yearly rhythms are called **circannual** for similar reasons.

Under experimental conditions of constant light, the circadian clocks of nocturnal animals are frequently delayed whilst those of day-active species are typically accelerated. These adaptations provide adjustment in nature to the change of seasons. In summer, day-active species need to wake up earlier each day, while nocturnal animals emerge later in the evening from their daytime retreats. These physiological adjustments to the animals' biological clocks are synchronised by the intensity and duration of the light period. In constant darkness the reverse occurs and the experimental animals adjust their biological clocks as they would, under natural conditions, in the autumn. We shall not, however, discuss the physiology of biological rhythms any further except in the context of their ecological significance (Figure 7.2).

The principal synchroniser for daily changes in Protista, Plantae, Fungi and Animalia is either the increase in light intensity that occurs at dawn or

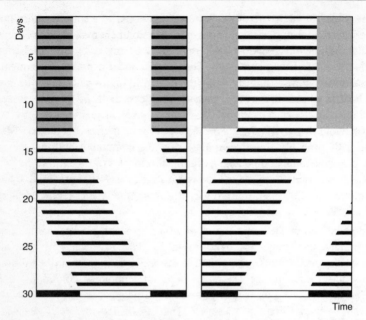

7.2   The times of locomotory activity of a generalised nocturnal animal (e.g. a mammal), left, and a generalised day-active animal (e.g. a lizard or bird), right, during a 12-day sojourn in a 24-hour light–dark regime followed by 17 days in constant illumination during which the organism typically adapts a free-running period either longer (left) or shorter (right) than 24 hours. Shaded areas indicate darkness. Horizontal lines show times of activity. The white strip indicates the light period from 06:00 to 18:00 hours (after F.A. Brown Jr).

the decrease at dusk. Day-active forms are usually stimulated by the former, nocturnal organisms by the latter. Light is the most usual and important synchroniser of diurnal rhythms, but temperature too may occasionally be effective. In nature, thermal influences probably reinforce and supplement those of light intensity. Cycles of daily, lunar or seasonal frequency ensure the preadaptation of living organisms to the forthcoming fluctuations of environmental conditions.

The leaves of the scarlet runner bean and other Leguminosae, as well as those of the telegraph plant (*Desmodium gyrans*), the sensitive plant (*Mimosa pudica*) and the fronds of certain ferns (*Marsilia*) change their positions at dusk and dawn. Many flowers open by day and close at night: light is responsible for the opening of the daisy and of the wood sorrel, but it causes the flowers of tobacco plants and the evening primrose to close. The ecological significance of this must be that the flowers are adapted to the periods of activity of the insects that pollinate them (Chapter 10). The most important function of the biological clocks of plants, however, is to measure day length. This is responsible for **photoperiodism**, the regulation flowering. In 1918, W.W. Garner and later H.A. Allard concluded that **long-day** plants flower when the photoperiod exceeds 12 to 14 hours, whilst **short-day** plants flower when it is below about 11 to 15 hours, depending upon the species. Some plants which do not respond to photoperiod are known as **day-neutral**. Photoperiodism ensures flowering at the appropriate period of the year.

Circadian rhythms

As far as animals are concerned, one of the main advantages of being able to measure the passage of time lies in the ability it confers to predict and be ready for the onset of daybreak or dusk. Many animals of the desert biome – scorpions, tarantulas, jerboas and kangaroo rats, for instance, are nocturnal. High daytime temperatures, the saturation deficiency of the atmosphere and predatory birds make it unsuitable for them to leave their burrows before it gets dark. The sooner they emerge after nightfall, however, the better it is for them. That is where their circadian clocks are invaluable because like alarm clocks they stimulate their owners into activity just at the right time.

Even in temperate biomes, most species of woodlice, centipedes, millipedes, springtails, fruit flies and so on are unable to withstand the high rate of total evaporation or **transpiration** (measured by loss in weight at various humidities) that they would have to endure were they in the open during the hours of daylight. So they come out at night to feed and find suitable mates. That, of course, is when many small nocturnal predators, alerted by their own biological clocks, tend also to appear. At the same time, daytime predators will have retired for the night, the darkness providing security from others. Rhythmicity has both physiological and ecological advantages.

Navigation

A second use for biological clocks lies in **time-compensated** solar and celestial navigation. You can only steer by the sun or the stars if you allow for their apparent movement across the sky. This involves the principle of the sun-compass used by Allied forces in the North African desert during the Second World War.

The ability of honeybees to return to a source of food at the same time each day has been known since the beginning of the twentieth century. They visit sources of nectar and pollen when these are most readily available. Thereby they achieve maximum productivity. Their ability to analyse the pattern of **polarised light** in the sky and to compensate for the movement of the sun enables honeybees to find their way to and from the hive at all times of the day. In polarised light, the vibrations in the light wave are confined to a single direction because many of the oscillations are thinned out into one place when light passes through the atmosphere. Time-compensated sun-compass orientation has also been described in locusts, beetles, pond skaters, sand hoppers, wolf spiders and other arthropods, amphibians, reptiles and mammals. It is especially important in the case of diurnal birds, while time-compensated orientation using the stars and allowing for their apparent movement in the sky is important to many migratory species which fly both by day and at night.

Circalunadian and seasonal rhythms

Many marine plants and animals show not only tidal rhythms but also bi-monthly or monthly circalunadian reproductive cycles in which all the members of a population within a particular region tend to become sexually active at the same time. This synchronisation is essential to the maintenance of the species because it ensures that the eggs and sperm are discharged in concentrations sufficiently high to provide a reasonable chance of fertilisation taking place and for some of the resulting embryos to survive.

Plants and animals have evolved many ways in which they are able to avoid or anticipate seasonal changes on Earth. Migration is just one of them. In order to become preadapted to the forthcoming season, however, their circannual clocks usually receive some synchronising signal from the environment. In most cases this is not the seasonal change in temperature and rainfall, but of day length which is measured by means of circadian clocks. Photoperiodic responses trigger the reproductive cycles and migrations of birds, as well as **hibernation** and **aestivation** (or summer dormancy) in a variety of other animals. The advantages of seasonal synchrony are, in many ways, similar to those of synchrony based on daily or lunar rhythms of activity.

An additional benefit accruing from synchronised reproduction is that the appetites of local predators become satisfied long before significant inroads have been made into the prey population, most of which thereby escape – at least for a while.

Until the advent of modern technology and the development of remotely controlled submersibles, it was assumed that the bottom of the deep seas was absolutely static and that a slow and steady rain of dead planktonic organisms fell continually, year in and year out, from the photic zone above. This is now known not to be the case. The growing season in the surface waters engenders a considerable amount of **phytodetritus** in the form of conglomerations of phytoplanktonic organisms that sink comparatively rapidly. The sudden appearance of this abundant food for the primary consumers signals the beginning of their breeding season. This, in turn, stimulates the secondary consumers to reproduce; but whether or not circannual clocks are involved is not known.

Succession, development and climax vegetation

Successional changes within a community leading towards a stable state or climax are known as **seres**. Seres are divided into two groups according to their origin. Those that occur in pristine environments – such as areas that have been very severely burned, volcanic islands immediately after their appearance, ploughed fields, recently stabilised sand dunes, newly created ponds and so on – are known as **primary succession**. **Secondary succession** is the term applied to the changes that occur when an established ecological community is disturbed so that it undergoes alterations in its structure. For instance, when primary rainforest is felled, the secondary forest that succeeds it consists of a much smaller number of different species of trees. Secondary succession does not necessarily follow the pattern of the primary succession. Indeed, it seldom if ever does so since both climatic and biotic factors will probably have changed since the original climax vegetation first evolved.

The distinction between primary and secondary succession is usually blurred, because the disturbances which destroy the fabric of a community and its systems' physical support vary in both extent and degree. A ploughed field represents a smaller, far less disturbed environment than does a volcanic island. Krakatoa (now known as Rakata) lies between Java and Sumatra. When it blew up in 1883, after a long period of repeated volcanic eruptions, at least half the island disappeared beneath the ocean and the remainder was covered by ash and pumice. The entire flora and fauna were obliterated, but primary succession took over and the island was recolonised surprisingly quickly. Within 25 years more than 100 species had established themselves. Subsequently, some of these disappeared and others took their places.

Primary succession can be observed in any newly created habitat although ecologists may not live long enough to witness the whole process. The first colonists consist of **pioneers** – species specially adapted to be good invaders. For example, fire is a natural environmental event in most parts of Australia, although it usually occurs at intervals of between 5 and 50 years or even longer. Not only have many plant species developed traits that enable them to persist after being burned, but others have evolved which actively exploit recently burned areas – as have numerous species of animals. Pioneers are eventually replaced by other species slower to exploit the new environment but which are more successful in the long run. Successional species themselves affect the environment by providing shade, contributing detritus to the soil and altering its moisture content. Such changes often inhibit the development of the very species that initiated them, thereby making the environment more suitable to their successors.

The transition of an abandoned field to mature forest in the deciduous forest biome proceeds through a number of vegetational stages. Pioneering annual plants quickly cover bare soil but, within a few years, they are replaced by perennial herbs and shrubs. In some regions, the shrubs are then followed by pine trees which crowd out the earlier successional species. Mature forests of pine are not the climax, however, although it may take a century or more before deciduous hardwood forest finally establishes itself as the natural climax vegetation of the biome.

Equilibrium theory

Equilibrium theories about diversity have dominated ideas on community organisation during the last three or four decades. Beginning with the mathematical analyses of the interactions of species pioneered at the beginning of the twentieth century by A.J. Lotka and V. Volterra and subsequently put to the test by Raymond Pearl and G.F. Gause in the 1920s (Chapter 6), ecologists came to realise that two species would not be able to coexist on a single limiting resource. Twenty years later, David Lack applied the concept of competitive interaction to the problems of ecologial conservation and, in the 1950s, G.E. Hutchinson developed the concept of **species packing** in multi-dimensional niche space. Finally, R.H. MacArthur and E.O. Wilson enunciated their **equilibrium theory** of island biogeography in 1967.

According to this theory, the number of species on islands balances regional processes governing immigration against local processes governing extinction. If islands are too small for new species to arise on them, the number of species they contain can only be increased by immigration from elsewhere. The greater the distance separating an island from sources of immigration, the fewer will be the species that inhabit it. The same applies to the number of species in mainland communities. Habitats become saturated by species whose numbers are determined by local ecologial conditions. The greater diversity of species found in the tropics compared with higher latitudes reflects the differences in resources and in the interactions between species so that more can coexist.

8 | PLANTS, PHYTOPHAGOUS INVERTEBRATES AND VERTEBRATE HERBIVORES

Up to this point in the book we have mainly been establishing the general synecological factors and principles that govern the populations of living organisms. From now on, we shall not only emphasise these in greater detail but will be entering the realm of evolutionary ecology and the interpretation of form and function in plants and animals as adaptations to their biotic environments. These adaptations can also be expressed in terms of heredity but, as has already been stated, genetics will not be discussed in this volume. The interactions between plants and their abiotic and edaphic environments were outlined in Chapter 2. In this chapter we shall concentrate upon the interactions and responses of plants to **phytophagous** (plant-eating) invertebrates and to larger herbivores – that is to say, the responses of autotropic producers to primary consumers – as well as on some of the interactions between plants and herbivores.

Phytophagous invertebrates

Marine herbivores

Various slugs and snails (Mollusca) feed on land plants, mainly at night, but they are not ecologically very important. Molluscs are more significant as herbivores both in fresh water and in marine environments, especially rocky shores where they browse on sea weeds and other algae. Nevertheless, although they play an important role in some food webs they are seldom if ever sufficiently numerous to have a marked influence on the total primary production of the oceans despite the fact that periwinkles, top shells and, especially, limpets may be very numerous locally and their influence on the vegetation is then considerable.

It has been estimated that, in their first year of life, some 75 cm^2 of encrusting weed is necessary for the maintenance of every cm^3 of limpet. If limpets are removed from an area of rock that is almost bare of sea weed as a result of their constant browsing, a succession begins in the course of which sea weeds such as *Enteromorpha*, *Porphyra* and *Ulva* soon become established. *Fucus* appears later and, once it has reached a certain size, cannot be eaten down. Were it not for the presence of limpets, the rocks would carry a much greater biomass of weed. At the same time, were reserves of sea weeds not abundant in other regions where they are too large to be eaten, there would be no constant replenishment of food for limpets.

Terrestrial invertebrate herbivores

By far the most important phytophagous invertebrates on land are insects and, to a lesser extent, other Arthropoda – the phylum containing the classes Crustacea, Arachnida and Insecta. Many marine crustaceans feed on algae but, of terrestrial forms, only woodlice (Isopoda) are sufficiently numerous to be of much ecological significance and, in any case, they feed mostly on humus and detritus.

Phytophagous mites

Of the arachnids, only some mites (Acari) are phytophagous. Many of the mites which we see on plants are in fact predators on sap-sucking insects. A few families of mites, however, have evolved mouth parts specialised for piercing plant cells and sucking out their contents. The withdrawal of these contents leaves white patches on the leaves, which later turn brown. There is also a tendency for heavily infected leaves to curl. Some acarine genera spin silk and cover the foliage with a light web beneath which the mites live. The European fruit tree red spider mite (*Metatetranychus ulmi*) does not spin a web. It is a serious pest of both soft and top fruit in the UK. This pest was initially created by human activity. Insecticides sprayed to control codlin moths (*Cydia pomonella*), whose larvae burrow into apples, virtually exterminated the natural predators and parasites of red spider mites which thereupon increased vastly in numbers.

The eggs of red spider mites overwinter in a state of diapause which cannot be broken by a rise in temperature unless, as A.D. Lees showed, they have previously been chilled to temperatures of 1 to 9 °C for at least 150 to 200 days. They hatch during April into larvae which begin feeding and, in about 12 days, produce the first generation of summer forms. The fifth generation, which arises in late summer or autumn, lays the winter eggs that enter diapause.

Some mites are ecologically important because they transmit the spores of pathogenic fungi and other organisms that cause diseases in plants. Others are pathogenic in themselves; the Eriophyidae, in particular, tend to cause galls and other malformations on their host plants. As in the case of insect-produced galls, those caused by eriophyid infection are characteristic in form for each particular species of mite.

Plants and insects

As we shall see later, the associations between plants and insects may be beneficial to both, but in most cases the insects obtain nourishment and the plants are injured, sometimes even to the extent of being defoliated. Every part of a plant, living or dead, can be utilised by insects – green leaves, pollen, seeds, fruit, sap, bark, wood and roots. Portions of leaves and bark are used to construct cocoons, cases or resting places. Some insects have mandibles for chewing, others have mouth parts adapted for sucking plant juices or sipping nectar. In this case the plant may benefit from being pollinated (Chapter 10). Many species of insects, including butterflies and moths (Lepidoptera), have larvae that feed on leaves while the adults subsist upon nectar. Not only are phytophagous insects adapted morphologically for eating leaves or boring into stems, but they are also adapted physiologically and behaviourally and equipped with the necessary sense organs for locating the appropriate plants on which to feed or lay their eggs.

Probably over half of all insect species feed directly upon plant material, both living or dead. Species that do not do so are carnivores or detritivores. Phytophagous insects include Hemiptera Homoptera (plant sucking bugs), larval Lepidoptera, Orthoptera excluding mantids (i.e. crickets and grasshoppers), and Ephemeroptera (mayfly) larvae, sawfly (Hymenoptera Symphyta) larvae, as well as the beetle (Coleoptera) families Chrysomelidae, Cerambycidae, Buprestidae, Elateridae and Curculionidae. Plant defences against such enemies include tough or hairy leaves, resins and toxic compounds of one kind or another.

Plant-eating insects

Different types of plant feeding have led to the evolution of different insect guilds, such as sap suckers, leaf miners, borers, gall makers, seed feeders and so on. A guild, it will be remembered, is an assemblage of species that use the environment in a similar way. In most cases, insects feed upon plants without killing them. There are few plants, other than the ginkgo and the tree of heaven (*Ailanthus*), that do not harbour numerous insect pests. Even poison ivy is host to leaf miners, pyralid moths and scolytid beetle larvae. A single species of plant may support many species of insect. Some 400 insect species have been recorded from apple trees, more than 150 from pines and 200 or more from corn. Oak trees are attacked by at least 1000 species of insects, of which 50 are leaf miners. Indeed, a single tree can support a thriving community (Chapter 2; Figure 2.5). Insects that are nutritionally restricted to a single plant species are said to be **monophagous**, those that attack only one or two plant species are **diphagous**, while species that attack many kinds of plants are called **polyphagous**. The latter are the most common (Figure 8.1).

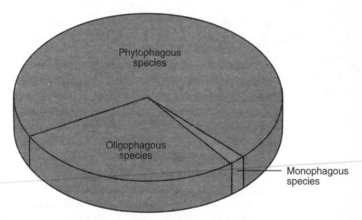

8.1 Typical relative pest status of different feeding types of phytophagous insects and mites.

Leaf miners

Leaf miners form a natural guild of insects, although they are not always related taxonomically. Their larvae feed for all or part of their existence between the two epidermal layers of a leaf. The mining habit converges on one hand with that of borers and gall makers, on the other with external feeders. Although most boring insects penetrate deeply into the tissues of their host plants some, such as the larvae of the codlin moth, may come to the surface occasionally and mine for a short distance just below the skin of an apple. Leaf mining has evolved in four insect orders: Lepidoptera (Figure 8.2), Coleoptera, Diptera and Hymenoptera. Like aquatic and subterranean insects, leaf miners occupy an ecological niche neglected by other animals. They may compete with one another but take their food differently. The damage they cause is therefore characteristic of each particular species. Their life histories are sometimes extremely complicated, but each mine often reveals the position of the egg, the type of feeding and number of moults.

8.2 Leaf mining moth caterpillar.

Leaf rollers

Insects distort plant leaves in different ways. Aphids and leaf hoppers may cause them to curl and pucker, but true **leaf rollers** are insects whose larvae spin silk which is used to twist and roll the leaf (Figure 8.3). There

8.3 Leaf rolled by moth caterpillar.

are several evolutionary steps in the development of leaf rolling. Many insects make use of leaves that are already curled, but only certain moth larvae, a few Coleoptera and sawflies, and one species of grasshopper roll leaves for themselves. The habit is often associated with special methods of feeding, the rolled leaves protecting their occupants to some extent from parasites. The leaf rolling grasshopper uses its case solely for protection and abandons it during the day time – surprisingly to feed upon aphids. (Most grasshoppers are phytophagous.) Some insects fold leaves at their edges instead of rolling them.

Gall makers

Plant **galls** can be produced by mechanical irritation, such as the rubbing of two branches in the wind, by fungal growth or attacks by nematodes, mites and insects (mainly Lepidoptera) (Figure 8.4). The presence of galls shows that a degree of reciprocity (Chapter 10) has begun to evolve between the causative agent and its plant host; and the production of galls is seldom harmful to the plant that produces them.

8.4 Woody gall caused by gall wasp.

Borers

In contrast to gall makers there is probably no group of insects more injurious to plants and more threatening to their survival than **borers**. The boring habit occurs mainly among Isoptera (termites), Coleoptera, Diptera, Hymenoptera and Lepidoptera. It has three functions: providing a source of food, a means of protection during the larval and pupal **instars** or stages of development and a place for rearing the brood in the case of social and subsocial species.

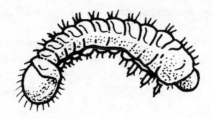

8.5 Larva of death-watch furniture beetle (much enlarged).

The larvae of boring insects are typically cylindrical in shape, legless, with reduced antennae and the head telescoped within the thorax (Figure 8.5). This development reaches its maximum in the larvae of buprestid and cerambycid beetles and those of wood wasps (Hymenoptera Siricidae). Species that bore into fruits or succulent plants have short life cycles with at least one generation a year, but those that bore into wood require at least two or three years in which to mature; while some timber beetles may need from 15 to 20 years when infesting seasoned hardwood. This extended period is caused by the lack of suitable nutrients and humidity. Very old wood is seldom attacked, and money spent on protecting the timbers of ancient buildings in temperate climates is usually wasted! In tropical regions, dead wood is almost invariably consumed by termites long before it becomes seasoned.

Reactions of plants to insects

The reactions of plants to phytophagous insects are by no means always negative. Some plants may even benefit indirectly from being eaten if they suffer less damage from it than their competitors do. The most important defences of plants against phytophagous insects are chemical. These are chiefly effective against vertebrate herbivores and will be discussed below. **Alkaloids** are found in approximately 20 per cent of angiosperm species, but many insects have evolved an immunity to alkaloid poisoning. Some even **sequester**, or store for their own defence, alkaloids from the plants on which they feed. Plants only invest enough resources in toxins and repellents to ensure that they are eaten less than their competitors. Some only produce toxic compounds when their leaves or those of neighbouring plants of the same species begin to be eaten by caterpillars. They are stimulated by air-borne chemicals. The floral biology of the higher plants coevolved with the insects. It is not surprising, therefore, that defences against phytophagous insects should have evolved simultaneously with the evolution of insects.

Phytophagous vertebrates

Marine herbivores

In addition to algae, sea grasses (*Thalassia*) are important plants on some coral reefs. Another name for them is turtle grasses because they are often grazed by green turtles (*Chelonia mydas*), one of the few strictly herbivorous species of reptiles in the world today. Most modern reptiles are generalist carnivores, foliage, fruits and flowers forming only a part of their diet. Green turtles normally graze on already grazed plots and continually crop the new growth. When introduced to new areas, they bite the sea grass close to its base, allowing the older fragments to float away and thus establish a large grazed pasture that can be harvested daily. Manatees are plant-eating mammals of tropical salt and fresh water around the Atlantic shores. Dugongs are their counterparts in the Indian Ocean and Australian seas.

Avoidance of herbivores on land

In the sea, the phytoplankton comprises the bulk of autotrophic producers but, on land, that role is assumed by gymnosperms and angiosperms. In desert regions, where vegetative life is relatively scarce, one of the not unexpected responses of plants to herbivores is as far as possible to avoid being eaten. This is achieved in two ways. Many species are active only when rain falls: at other times of the year they remain hidden as spores or seeds in aestivaton buried beneath the surface of the sand. When rain falls, they germinate and grow extremely rapidly. The whole life cycle is compressed into a few weeks, in recognition of which such plants are often termed **ephemerals**. As they all appear almost simultaneously, herbivorous insects and vertebrates are provided with so much food that they become satiated without making heavy inroads into their source of nutrition. Other desert plants endure the dry season by remaining underground in the form of bulbs, corms, or roots. Even so, they may well be dug up and devoured.

Plant camouflage

Those desert plants that remain on the bare soil surface may escape notice by means of **camouflage** or **protective resemblance**. For instance, some succulents produce sticky hairs on their surfaces which trap particles of dust and sand so that they are concealed from the gaze of larger herbivores such as gazelles and camels. Other succulents escape as a result of their resemblance to stones. This phenomenon is extensively developed in the arid regions of southern Africa and is also encountered in Somalia, Ethiopia and North America. The plants concerned usually do not merely resemble just any stone or rock. They duplicate the shape, size, colour, texture and fracture lines of the particular rock substrate of the habitat to which they are restricted. Sometimes the entire plant lies buried with only the tips of the leaves exposed as in the stone plant *Lithops salicola* (Figure 8.6) of the Kalahari and certain soil cacti of the northern Atacama desert of Chile. Although the advantages of dwelling beneath the soil surface may lie mostly in the reduction of water loss through transpiration, avoidance of the attention of grazing herbivores is also beneficial. The resemblance to stones is certainly not fortuitous.

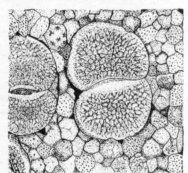 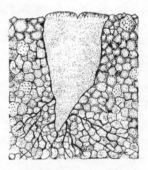

8.6   Stone plant, *Lithops salicola*. Right, diagram of growth form; left, close-up of expanded leaves.

Some edible succulents of arid and semi-arid regions of Somalia, southern and eastern Africa have wrinkled, greyish stems and grow inconspicuously among the weathered branches of dead shrubs. Others resemble the droppings of geese, gazelles, antelope or camels, and consequently also escape being grazed. Not only is mimicry chracteristic of the succulent plants of arid regions, but it also occurs among the mistletoes (Loranthaceae) of arid Australia which, to some extent, resemble their less palatable host plants and thereby escape being selected by leaf-eating possums (*see* Chapter 10).

Deterrence of herbivores

Like phytophagous insects, vertebrate herbivores may be deterred by the presence of distasteful or poisonous chemicals in the vegetation that they might otherwise eat. Most current work on the anti-herbivore systems of plants assumes a cost, associated with the production and maintenance of a given level of defence against both invertebrate pests, mainly insects, and browsing and grazing vertebrates. This cost is often expressed as a loss in productive growth. For example, the synthesis of 10 per cent L-canavanine in plant seeds can protect them against most seed-eating beetles (Bruchidae). Consequently, the expenditure of resources and energy in providing the enzymes for canavanine metabolism are a sound economic investment, costing the plant less than it would to produce additional seeds to compensate for the losses inflicted by beetles in the absence of L-canavanine. This economic argument applies not only to defensive chemicals but also to structures such as thorns and spines, as well as to other kinds of costly activity in plants, including the production of nectar and of advertising structures including flowers, berries and fruits.

Effects of herbivory

Regrowth is a generalised response of plants to any type of damage, not only that caused by herbivores. Rapid regrowth may have been selected by any one of a large number of factors or, more probably, by a combination of all of them. There is no reason to assume that the increases in productivity which occasionally follow herbivory constitute a specific evolutionary response to herbivory, as has sometimes been suggested in the past. Indeed, there is no evolutionary justification and little actual evidence to support the idea that plant–herbivore mutualisms should evolve. None of the assumptions that underlie discussions of the benefits of herbivory are necessarily correct and there is no compelling evidence that herbivory actually increases plant fitness. On the contrary, it is often highly deleterious, sometimes less so but generally harmful nevertheless although, as already mentioned, it may afford a competitive advantage. The system is one of costs and benefits (see below).

Despite the fact that they provide the basic source of food for all animal and microbial life, plants are not usually consumed to the point at which they are no longer able to support the organisms that depend upon them. Much ecological research has been undertaken on the mechanisms that determine the balance between maintaining population numbers and not over-exploiting the resources of the habitat. Nevertheless, plants are sometimes severely affected by plant-eating animals, both directly and indirectly. Thus, seed production is extremely sensitive to attack on the leaves by herbivores and reduced seed production is typically the first response of a plant to defoliation.

Unpalatability

Many plants owe their unpalatability to secondary metabolites; but no defence can be perfect and a balance is usually achieved through the interaction of numerous factors. Moreover, individual plants may vary their resistance to the ill effects of browsing. Plants obtain chemical protection from herbivorous animals mainly through the secretion of **secondary** repellent and toxic chemicals. Secondary compounds can be defined as those which do not function directly in the primary biochemical activities that support growth, development and reproduction of the organism in which they occur. In the case of plants, they are of importance in interactions between plants and animals and between plants and microorganisms, as well as between plants and other plants. No less than morphological features, they are subject to the selective pressures of the environment. Probably millions of secondary compounds have been synthesised by plants in the course of their evolution, and those that increased the competitive fitness of the plant in which they arose have survived. The secondary metabolites that make plants unpalatable, toxic or repellent to herbivorous animals include:

1 alkaloids
2 toxic amino acids
3 toxic amines and peptides
4 toxic proteins
5 cyanogenic glycosides and nitro-glycosides
6 coumarin glycosides
7 steroid and triterpenoid glycosides
8 irritant oils
9 organic acids

10 phenolic acids and tannins
11 volatile oils.

The nitrogen content of the vegetation is a limiting nutritional factor for many herbivorous animals. Those that are adapted to feed on plants with low nitrogen contents have low growth rates and long life cycles. Plants that are rich in nitrogen suffer the severest attack, especially from insects, not merely because they are nutritionally rich but because they can support species with rapid growth and short life cycles.

Costs of defence

The cost of defensive compounds, in terms of reduced growth due to the allocation of carbon and energy for their production, varies according to the rate of photosynthesis and the proportion of leafage allocated for this purpose. For this reason, qualitative defences are mainly found in plants with lower photosynthetic rates. When diverted from growth and metabolic functions to defence, the cost in terms of nitrogen is highest in plants with low nitrogen contents as well as low photosynthetic rates. Consequently, nitrogenous defence compounds are found only in plants with high nitrogen contents. Where soil nutrients are in short supply, it is cheaper to produce carbon-based defence compounds. Even with higher concentrations of available nitrogen, it is more expensive to produce tannins than other chemical defensive substances.

Antifeedants

While feeding, insects secrete **hormones** or **endocrines** which stimulate their digestive processes. Hormones are regulatory substances, active at low concentrations, that engender physiological responses of various kinds. Some compounds not only fail to stimulate feeding, however, but actually discourage it. These chemicals are known as **antifeedants** and, not surprisingly, many of them are synthesised by plants and disrupt the endocrine systems of the insects that attempt to feed on them. Some inactivate the digestive enzymes of insects, some operate in the same way as the hormone that controls insect development, while others act like the reproductive hormones of birds and mammals. Many plants employ **induced defences** which, as mentioned above, are activated only after attack. In this way the cost to the plants of producing these secondary metabolites is reduced to a minimum.

Epidermal defences of plants

The defences of plants against herbivores include impregnation of the epidermis with lignin, silica, cork or wax so that the tissue cannot easily be bitten or chewed. Other epidermal defences include hairs, glands and spines. Some plant surfaces are even endowed with structures which look like insect eggs and therefore deter ovipositing insects, but none of them renders its possessor completely free from attack. Spines deter large herbivores, mainly by causing them pain – the mouth, nose and eyes being especially sensitive. Some spines are reinforced by venoms. The hairs of stinging nettles would be little deterrent were they not poisonous. Sharp, clean punctures and tears cause less pain than do ragged wounds. Recurved spines, including those of the wait-a-bit thorn (*Acacia mellifera*) of the Namib desert, camel thorn (*A.erioloba*), the North American catclaw acacia (*A.greggii*) and ironwood trees (*Olneya tesota*), for example, impale the flesh of moving animals. Their curvature causes the spines to penetrate deeper as the animal pulls away. Barbed spines, including those of cacti, especially the prickly pear (*Opuntia*), cause intense pain in humans. These barbs are adapted so that they become firmly attached to the tough, elastic integuments of mammals and birds, and the oral tissues of lizards. Many cacti have thin, membranous sheaths around their spines (Figure 8.7), the function of which is not known. Perhaps they protect the spines from becoming clogged with dust.

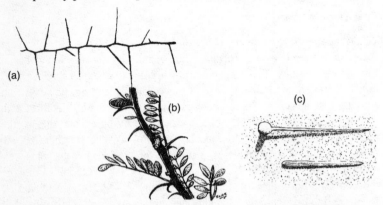

8.7 Plant spines: (a) piercing spines of *Zizyphus obtusifolia*; (b) recurved spines of ironwood (*Olneya phaecantha*); (c) *Opuntia* spine with the sheath removed.

Plant–herbivore interactions

The interactions between plants and herbivorous animals are far from static. On the contrary, physical and biochemical evolutions are continually taking place. There is a trade-off between processes of growth and **differentiation** which interact with herbivory and inter-plant competition. (Differentiation means the occurrence of changes in structure and function due to increased specialisation.) For example, two aspects of the evolution of typical African plants seem to have been influenced by giraffes and extinct browsers – the presence of large thorns and spines on many plants and the characteristic flat-topped shape of savanna acacia trees. Thorns, spines and hooks are also charcteristic of other African trees that are browsed by giraffes. It seems probable that spines have evolved as a result of browsing by mammals because, in Australia which lacks large browsing animals, the trees are without thorns. Thorns are longer at lower levels where African acacia trees are heavily browsed by goats and antelopes, than they are higher up where only giraffes can reach.

Anyone who has landed at Nairobi airport will have noticed the large brown swellings at the bases of the thorns of the acacia trees which are so common in that region of Kenya. These swellings are inhabited by large numbers of ants, while the swollen spines of the white whistling thorn trees are inhabited by other insects. Although the ants do not cause these swellings to appear, they hollow them out by their constant activity. Many **myrmecophytes**, or plants that are associated with ants, bear special structures for housing ants, and most are also furnished with **foliar nectaries** or other fruit bodies that are exploited by insects (Figure 8.8a).

Despite the wide range of species of mulga trees of the genus *Acacia* in arid Australia, myrmecophytic structures have not been evolved in that continent and, as we have seen, thorns have either not evolved, or have been lost (Figure 8.8c). In contrast, Afro-Asian species are very spiny or are strongly myrmecophytic. This is correlated with the presence of large and effective faunas of browsing mammals, both now and in the recent geological past (Figure 8.8b). Ants tend to concentrate at the short tips which are preferred by grazing herbivores. Furthermore, the thorns of myrmecophytic species of acacia are shorter than those of species without ants, suggesting a trade-off between ants and thorns as defences. Other aspects of **mutualism** – the relationship between two species which benefits both parties – will be discussed in Chapter 10.

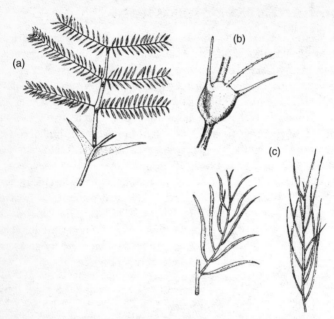

8.8 Leaves and spines of acacias. (a) a species with folia nectaries and other fruit bodies that are exploited by ants. (b) stipular spines of another species with bases swollen to form a nest chamber for ants. (c) leafy tips of an Australian mulga tree showing absence of thorns. (Not to scale.)

9 | PREDATORS AND PREY

Predation is a factor of the utmost ecological importance. It is the link that joins secondary, tertiary, and higher levels of consumption to that of the primary consumers in the flow of energy through the various ecosystems. In the previous chapter, we analysed the link between primary consumers and producers and saw how each affected the other. Likewise on an evolutionary scale, predators react mutually with their prey. Natural selection, generated by competition between predators for food and heavy selection on their prey to avoid being eaten, leads to an 'arms race' between predator and prey, the factors limiting which are physical, physiological and cost-effectiveness. Moreover all animals, even top predators at the summit of their ecological pyramids of numbers and biomass, are, at some stages of their life cycles, potential prey for other predators. Consequently, their adaptations represent compromises between being efficient both at hunting and in escaping capture.

Adaptations of predatory carnivores

Predators need to capture and kill their prey before they can eat it. They do this in different ways using a variety of weapons – the scorpion's sting, the spider's web, the raptatorial legs of the praying mantis, the arms of the octopus, the concealment and venom of the horned viper, the flight and stoop of the falcon and the stalking of a lion or tiger.

Successful predation involves at least five separate processes:

1 Detection of the prey as an object distinct from its environment;
2 Its identification despite concealment, disguise or mimicry;
3 Approach in such a way that the prey does not escape by flight;
4 Subjugation of the prey although it may have weapons of its own, armour and other anti-predator defences;
5 Finally, its consumption.

Some predators seek their prey actively by searching for it, others lie in wait – sometimes in disguise – and ambush it.

Certain predatory types, such as vultures, scarcely catch living prey at all, but have secondarily adopted a scavenging mode of life. Combinations of predatory techniques are frequently employed, while many predators, including lions, hyenas, foxes and bears alternate predation with scavenging according to whatever potential sources of nourishment they may come upon. Finally, many animals are **omnivores** feeding on both plant and animal food. Human beings are omnivores, as are pigs, chimpanzees and dogs, as well as many birds and reptiles. Omnivores are ecologically unusual in that they operate over a range of trophic levels.

Hunting methods

Many predatory animals hunt by **speculation** in that they wander, apparently at random, until they come by chance upon suitable prey which they detect by sight, scent, sound or touch. Octopuses use their arms to feel for crabs in rocky crevices. Herons stir up mud and debris with one foot and spear fleeing fishes with their beaks. Lions and cheetahs stalk prey that they have detected by sight or smell as they wander across their territories.

Carmine bee-eaters ride on the backs of browsing goats or sheep, flying off to catch grasshoppers and other insects that have been disturbed, while tanagers and other neotropical birds follow army ants to snatch up any insects that have been flushed out by the ant columns.

Many predators stalk their prey until they are close enough to attack with a reasonable chance of success. They are frequently aided by the possession of concealing or **cryptic** coloration and move slowly, making skilful use of whatever cover is available. This is true not only of vertebrate predators, but also of invertebrates such as spiders, mantids and octopuses. Others lie in wait, completely concealed until the prey comes by chance within range. Crypsis is achieved by a combination of camouflage and stillness. In some cases the prey is attracted by movements of part of the body, such as the lure of an angler fish or the tail of a desert viper.

Ambush predators, which lie in wait for their prey, not infrequently position themselves so that they can see the prey clearly silhouetted against a light background. This is true, for instance, of sharks and groupers (Mycteroperca), while nightjars dart upwards at dusk to snap up insects visible against the pale night sky. Ambushing may be assisted by various auxiliary devices such as webs, sticky threads, pits and traps.

Some predators make use of **disguise** or **aggressive mimicry** in approaching their prey. Hawks may fly in the manner of jays when approaching unsuspecting sparrows and blennies (*Aspidonotus*) mimic cleaning wrasses (*Labroides*) in their coloration and movements so that they can get close enough to bite the fish that invites them to clean it.

Different families of large terrestrial carnivores have evolved typical hunting techniques to which they are morphologically adapted – dogs (Canidae) to swift and prolonged running which demands great stamina; cats (Felidae) to a concealed approach followed by a quick dash. Hyaenas (Hyaenidae) are coursers like dogs, both killing and scavenging on a wide variety of prey animals. They have extremely strong teeth and jaw muscles for crushing bones. Contrary to earlier belief it is now thought that carnivores tend to hunt in groups because they live in groups and not because they necessarily hunt cooperatively or experience greater foraging returns per capita than solitary individuals do. Nevertheless, the chances of escape must be reduced when a large prey animal, such as a wildebeest, is surrounded by a group of wild dogs or hyaenas.

Switching prey

Some predators are **monophagous** and specialise on a single species of prey. This is somewhat unusual, however, and most carnivorous animals exploit varied sources of food, and select balanced diets according to their needs. Mosquitoes provide a familiar example. Females need to suck blood in order to obtain sufficient protein for the development of their eggs. Males, on the other hand, only require carbohydrates to supply their energy requirements. Consequently they can obtain all the food and moisture they need from dew and nectar, leaving human beings and other animals in peace.

As most pet owners know, many captive animals appear to become bored with their food, unless offered occasional changes of diet. This applies not only to mammals and caged birds, but also to reptiles and aquarium fishes. In the wild, a clan of spotted hyenas may hunt wildebeest for some weeks and then suddenly switch to zebras or gazelles and later back to wildebeest. Moreover, different clans show preferences for different prey which cannot be explained by its availability in the respective clan ranges. Another factor of ecological significance is that the sizes of hyena groups vary with different prey. Hyenas hunt wildebeest or Thomson's gazelles either singly or in packs of two or three but, when hunting zebra, their packs may number up to 27 with an average of 10 or 11 animals.

Vertebrate predation usually increases as a function of the density of the prey. When these two parameters are plotted against one another in experimental populations, a sigmoid curve is obtained. In nature, however, when the prey species becomes scarce, predators usually switch to another type of prey before the first has been exterminated. **Frequency-dependent** predation refers to the fact that predators select a particular prey in proportion to the number of times that they encounter it. This could result from the fact that absolute predation rates on each prey type respond independently to changes in the density of that prey species. Alternatively, absolute predation rates on a particular type of prey could respond to more complex interactions between the density of that prey and the densities of other types of prey in the environment. Consequently, the frequency as well as the density of the prey becomes important. In practice it is difficult to differentiate between the two, but it seems probable that, except in very simple ecological relationships, predation rates depend upon a complex interaction between the prey's own density, other prey densities, and the diversity of prey in the environment.

Scavenging

Scavengers form an important link in numerous food chains. In the East African savanna, many predatory carnivores readily scavenge from the kills of other species. Vultures compete both among themselves and other animals for a share of the same carcass and the dead bodies of large mammals are scavenged by a succession of vultures. First to arrive are large, aggressive species with heavy skulls and beaks adapted for tearing flesh from bones and eating skin. Others with lighter skulls then thrust their heads deep into the carcasses and tear off soft flesh, while smaller species with thin bills pick up scraps, or strip shreds of skin from narrow spaces which the heavier bills of the larger species cannot reach. Lions and hyenas often scavenge from each other's prey. Lions tend to hunt during the day and scavenge at night, while hyenas more often hunt in groups at night and scavenge during the day.

After the largest scavengers have completed their grisly work, smaller species, followed by beetles, fly maggots and microorganisms ensure that nothing edible remains. This succession has no true climax because the scavengers disperse when everything has been eaten. They are, however, part of a climax which is, in fact, the entire savanna community.

Primary defences of prey

Predation is one of the strongest selective factors in most ecobiomes of the world and many animals have evolved anti-predatory devices. These can be divided into two main types; **primary** and **secondary**. Primary devices are defined as those which operate regardless of whether a predator is in the vicinity or not. They reduce the chances of an encounter between predator and prey and include living in a burrow or hole, protective coloration and the avoidance of detection by sight or sound. Secondary anti-predator devices are called into play only when a potential predator is present (see below).

Anachoresis

Many otherwise defenceless animals spend almost their entire lives hidden in crevices, beneath bark or in holes in the ground. Such recluses are known as **anachoretes** (from the Greek word meaning 'one who has withdrawn himself from the world'). It must be remembered, however, that even anachoretes may need to emerge in order to feed or mate. Most of them are lie-in-wait or sit-and-wait ambush predators and, like many burrowing spiders, dart from their lairs to capture prey. Even anachoretes, however, may be dug up and eaten, a fate that often befalls worms, centipedes, scorpions and beetle larvae, not to mention naked mole-rats!

Burrows and retreats

Many small animals secrete themselves for much of the time in burrows or retreats which help to shelter them from the attentions of predatory animals. Woodlice shelter from predatory birds, as well as from heat and dry air, under bark and beneath rocks and fallen logs. So do many other arthropods. Solitary Hymenoptera comprise mainly burrowing forms. Some solitary wasps dig individual nests in the ground, others dig communal nests or burrows with lateral chambers. Many reptiles, a few birds, including sand martens and bee-eaters, and small mammals such as mice, shrews, rats, rabbits and foxes, dig burrows for themselves or use those of other animals. An example, frequently cited, is the elf owl of the Sonoran desert which occupies holes excavated in saguaro cacti by the Gila wood pecker (Figure 9.1)

9.1   Elf owl occupying the hole in a saguaro cactus excavated by a Gila woodpecker.

Concealment

Most herbivorous animals, other than large species such as elephants, rhinoceroses and hippopotamuses, tend to have cryptic coloration so that they escape the attention of predators. Many smaller carnivores are also cryptic because they, too, have predatory enemies, while the concealing coloration of larger, well-defended predators may have an aggressive function enabling them to approach their prey unobserved.

The basic type of camouflage is best seen in relatively homogeneous environments such as tropical rainforest or desert, where the general coloration is relatively constant. The inhabitants of such environments are often coloured uniformly so that they match their backgrounds. Furthermore, a camouflaged animal may be thrown into relief by the effects of light and shade which enable the eye to detect curves and textures. This can be overcome by **countershading** which eliminates the appearance of roundness. Most animals are pale on their ventral surface and darker in colour on their backs and sides. Shadows are also eliminated behaviorally by flattening the body and facing the source of light.

The surface outline or contour of an animal may sometimes be concealed by **disruptive coloration** – a superimposed pattern of contrasted colours and tones which breaks up the surface outline as do the body stripes of many insects, fishes, frogs, reptiles, birds and mammals. Despite their size, both zebras and giraffes may become completely invisible even at close range in quite thin tree cover, although they are extremely conspicuous in open country. Again, the black head and shoulders of the Malayan tapir are very conspicuous in a museum or zoo, but they contrast with the white body to break up the animal's shape and make it unrecognisable in the rainforests of Indonesia and Malaysia. The significance of any form of adaptive coloration can only be considered in relation to the normal environment of its possessor.

Because of its regular shape, very few natural objects are more conspicuous than the vertebrate eye. It is a mark by which predators would readily detect camouflaged prey unless it were well concealed. Many fishes, amphibians, reptiles, birds and mammals have eyes with black, staring pupils which require special treatment if they are not to prejudice the success of the whole colour scheme of the animals. One of the methods most commonly used is to conceal the eye by means of a black disruptive line or **eye stripe**. In the common frog, for example, a blackened stripe level with the top of the pupil extends over the iris and continues across the skin at the side of the head. This disguises the eye by incorporating it into the eye stripe. Similar eye stripes appear in a variety of other animals and are especially common in fishes and snakes (Figure 9.2).

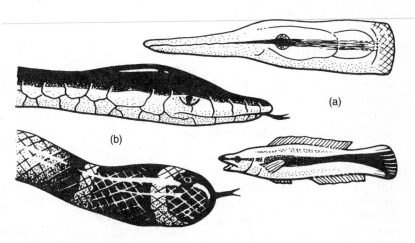

9.2 Camouflage and concealment of the eye in (a) fish, and (b) snakes.

Colour change

The chameleon is best known to many people because of its ability to change colour so that it matches its surroundings, but it is in no way unique in the possession of this facility. Several other kinds of lizards can do the same as can amphibians and many species of fish, crustaceans, stick insects, and cephalopods. As with other forms of crypsis, colour change may be used in defence as well as offence.

Physiological colour change is temporary and reversible. Colour resemblance may also show **seasonal dimorphism**. Various insect species that have more than one annual brood exhibit seasonal dimorphism; the colours of successive broods are correlated with the seasonally changing colours of the environment. With northern birds and mammals a similar end is achieved by seasonal changes in the feathers or hair respectively. Ptarmigan, willow grouse, mountain hares, foxes and stoats, for instance, change to white as winter approaches. In the early summer when the ice begins to melt and only small patches of snow remain, the ptarmigan moults the first of its white feathers. The remainder, nestling among the new dark feathers that have appeared, render the bird extremely inconspicuous in its temporarily variegated environment. All the white feathers are shed by the time most of the snow patches have melted.

Materials for camouflage

Many of the defences found in the animal kingdom serve their possessors in more ways than one. A wide variety of animals camouflage their bodies with materials taken from their environments. The sticks, pebbles or sand grains that various species of caddis-fly larvae use to clothe their bodies have a dual function. Not only do they disguise their possessors but, at the same time, they make them distasteful to many potential predators. Even so, several species of fishes rely on caddis larvae for their food, so there must be heavy selection on the larvae to build effective shields.

The terrestrial equivalent of caddis cases are constructed by the larvae of bag-worm moths (Psychidae). These build protective cases of silk to which twigs, leaves and fragments of vegetable matter are attached. They do not make new cases at every moult, but enlarge the original one as they grow. Many other kinds of insects also conceal themselves with adventitious material. For instance, some species of lace-wings cover their backs with dead ants; others which feed on woolly alder aphids cover their backs with waxy material taken from their prey. If the waxy material is removed with a paint brush, the lace-wing larvae are immediately attacked by the ants that normally guard the aphids. Several marine animals, such as crabs and other crustaceans, cover themselves with seaweed and, if moved to a new habitat, promptly change their disguise so that they cannot be detected.

Disguise and mimicry

Disguise or protective resemblance, in which a plant or animal looks like an inedible stick or stone that is of no significance to herbivores or potential predators, is widespread in nature. For disguise to be successful it is essential for a prey animal to remain motionless like the object that it resembles. Indeed, all forms of mimicry depend upon the mimic behaving like, as well as looking like, its **model**. The selective process involved is probably the same as that which produces true **mimicry**, of which there are two kinds, batesian and mullerian. In classical **batesian mimicry** (first described by H.W. Bates in 1862), a harmless and vulnerable species resembles an unpalatable or dangerous model that is ignored by potential predators. Harmless hover flies are often cited as mimics of venomous wasps or bees, bombardier beetles are mimicked by grasshoppers, ants by spiders, poisonous moths by harmless species and so on. It is not uncommon, especially in the tropics, for slow or flightless insects like some beetles to mimic speedy, agile insects such as flies, that are scarcely worth chasing. This phenomenon is known as **speed mimicry**.

Batesian mimicry is similar to disguise or protective resemblance in that it is a means of deceiving enemies. Whereas anachoresis and crypsis can prevent a predator from detecting its prey, disguise, mimicry and **aposematic** or warning coloration (see below) merely ensure that the prey is either not recognised as anything edible or else is regarded as something positively to be avoided. A noxious species benefits from warning coloration or sounds, because some of its members are sacrificed, or have to defend themselves, in teaching would-be predators to avoid them. Therefore, if one or more aposematic species mimic one another, the losses in teaching enemies not to attack them are shared and proportionately reduced.

The mimicry of one distasteful model by another distasteful species is known as **müllerian mimicry**. This was first described by F. Müller in 1878. Müllerian mimicry between aposematic species is beneficial, not only to potential prey which sacrifice fewer of their numbers in teaching potential predators to avoid them, but also to the predators themselves. It reduces the educational burden, allowing them to learn to avoid two or more unpalatable species with less effort than would be needed if the prey did not look alike. Aposematism is not restricted to colour alone: warning scents, sounds and threatening or **deimatic** displays are also aposematic.

Integument, scales and armour

Arthropods have hardened exoskeletons which protect them from attack by small predators. Large marine crustaceans such as lobsters and crabs are safe from many large enemies, although they are preyed on extensively by octopuses. The Cephalopoda, which includes octopuses and squids, is the only class of Mollusca to lack a protective shell. Starfish (Echinodermata) feed extensively on fish, crustaceans (including barnacles), worms, snails and bivalve molluscs. When a mussel is eaten it is held under the mouth of the starfish whose arms can pull on its valves with a force strong enough to lift 1350 g. The bivalve can withstand a greater force for a short time, but eventually yields to the sustained pull, accompanied by the digestive action of the stomach which is everted and applied against it. Starfish themselves are protected from most predators by the calcareous, bony **ossicles** bound together in the connective tissue underlying the epidermis.

On land, many insects are protected from smaller enemies including other insects, spiders and scorpions by hairs or spines. The fine, detachable scales on the wings of butterflies and moths are effective protection against attack by many kinds of spiders. They enable the insects to slip between the spiders' jaws or **chelicerae**. Some beetles have such hard integuments that they are protected from vertebrate predators as large as birds, shrews and mice. In addition, they are often distasteful. The scales of reptiles are protective as, to a much greater extent, are the shells of tortoises and turtles. Reptilian scales are composed of **keratin**. This is the name given to a group of fibrous proteins which form the structural bases of hair, wool, nails and other epidermal structures. The keratin of reptile scales is continually being rubbed away and renewed by the epidermal tissues beneath. Among lizards and snakes, it is sloughed at intervals, sometimes several times a year. In some lizards, the dermal parts of the scales contain small, horny **osteoderms** which make the skin exceedingly tough. In the head region, these plates may be attached to the underlying bones.

Girdle-tailed lizards (Cordylidae) of southern Africa have developed a remarkable armour of spines. Not only does this armour make them difficult for their potential predators to swallow, but it enables them to wedge themselves into crevices from which it is extremely difficult to extricate them. Spines are also accentuated in spiny lizards of various kinds. In these, the tail is a formidable defensive weapon. Indeed, second to teeth, tails are possibly the most effective weapons of defence amongst reptiles. They are employed with special effect by monitors (Varanidae), large iguanids and agamids.

Secondary defences of prey

Secondary anti-predator devices are invoked only in the presence of an enemy. The simplest response of most prey animals is to fly or run away, while burrowing forms withdraw as fast as they can into their shelters or retreats. This may not always be possible, however, and then self-defence, with whatever weapons are available, may become necessary. Some animals, such as tortoises or porcupines, are so well endowed with defences that they stand their ground and make no attempt whatever to escape. Others, equipped with formidable offensive weapons – especially powerful or venomous teeth – readily employ them for defence.

Thanatosis

Animals that are unable to evade their predators sometimes appear to 'give up' and become motionless, as though they were dead. Death feigning or **thanatosis** can inhibit attack because the prey fails to release a killing response in its predator. The best known example of this is seen in the American opossum from which we get the expression 'to play possum'. Many insects of various kinds also become inert when they are attacked, either with the limbs extended, or withdrawn close to the body so that they cannot be bitten off.

Death feigning is advantageous to an animal that cannot escape because many predators, including mantids, lizards, and cats, strike only at prey which shows signs of life. Some snakes roll themselves into tight, motionless balls which protect their vulnerable heads when they are attacked while the African savanna monitor adopts a rigid posture when it feigns death. Birds also employ thanatosis as a life-saving response and have been known to collapse suddenly in flight and fall to the ground.

More usual, however, is injury feigning, but this is employed not as a protection from its protagonist but as a means of distracting the attention of the predator from the eggs or young. Stone curlews, for instance, feign injury with remarkable realism when predators invade their nesting areas. Death feigning is not peculiar to the opossums. It is occasionally practised by other mammals including foxes and squirrels.

Deflection of attack

When attacked by a predator, a prey animal can sometimes escape by inducing its enemy to attack it in the wrong place. Diversion behaviour directs attack away from the vulnerable eggs or young and, in birds, may be achieved by injury feigning, while deflection marks induce predators to attack non-vulnerable parts of the body where little harm is caused. A classic example of this is seen in the small eyespots on the wings of many species of butterflies. These have long been known to deflect the attacks of birds from the vulnerable bodies of the insects. This hypothesis was confirmed in 1941 by G.D.H. Carpenter who noted that the beak marks on the wings of African butterflies were concentrated around the eyespots. Since these spots are normally near the edges of the wings, rather than near the body, the attacks had not been fatal.

Autotomy

When attacked by a predator, many insects and arachnids voluntarily sever or **autotomise** the limb that has been grasped and, thereby, make their escape. The missing leg is then regenerated at the next moult. Autotomy of the claws occurs in some Crustacea. Only the tails of reptiles can be sacrificed in this way and autotomy is not found in birds or mammals.

Spines and urticating hairs

Spines and **urticating** or stinging hairs are used in both primary and secondary defence. Hedgehogs are successful animals, not least on account of their spines. When threatened, they roll themselves into tight balls so that their heads, short legs, and underparts are protected. Porcupines charge backwards at their enemies. Their hind quarters are heavily armed with backward pointing spines which easily become detached from the body. When lodged in the flesh of a predator, they cannot easily be extracted and may occasionally even be fatal. The Australian equivalent is the egg-laying spiny ant-eater or echidna.

Barbed urticating hairs are characteristic of the larvae of Lepidoptera. Single or aggregated secretory cells pour their products onto them so that, when the hairs are embedded in the skin of a potential predator, their toxic contents are released subcutaneously. The urticating hairs of tarantula spiders may cause considerable irritation of the skin, but they are not toxic. They are actively combed by the hind legs into the faces of small mammalian predators. Tarantula keepers need to be careful not to let these hairs get into their eyes or delicate mucous membranes.

Venoms and toxins

Venomous animals include jellyfishes, corals, sea anemones, marine worms, sea urchins, spiders, scorpions, wasps, bees and ants, shrews and, above all, poisonous snakes. Venoms may be used both in defence and offence. In many animal taxa their original function was that of killing and digesting prey. Adult wasps use venom to kill the insects on which they rear their young and, only secondarily, in defence. They, themselves, feed on nectar. In contrast, bees are vegetarian in all stages of their life cycle and the sting is used for defensive purposes only. The stings of ants are used both in defence and in offence as are those of scorpions and the venoms of spiders.

Sting-fish, such as weevers, sting-rays and scorpion fishes, secrete venoms that cause intense pain to human beings unfortunate enough to be stung by one of their poisonous spines. People stung by the toad-fish (*Synanceia*) have been known to become delirious with the agony, hurling themselves about and even amputating the injured limb themselves. Fainting and collapse often occur, sometimes followed by death. Why such a formidable animal should also be extremely cryptic is difficult to understand. We need to discover the agent of natural selection against which the venom has been evolved. The same is true of venomous snakes, by no means all of which are aposematic.

As well as fishes with localised venoms there are numerous others whose flesh is toxic. In many cases these have acquired or sequestered their poisons through feeding on some organism, vegetable or animal, which is not toxic to the fish but which produces in its flesh a substance toxic to other animals. Before leaving the subject of dangerous fish, it is worth pointing out that electric fishes can produce violent shocks, both in defence and also to stun their prey.

The toxins of fishes are not dissimilar to those found in the skins of poison frogs (Dendrobatidae). Unlike most amphibians, these small frogs are among the most conspicuous animals in the world and, at the same time, the most toxic. In Colombia, Indian hunters tip their blowgun darts with the extremely poisonous alkaloids secreted by them. Many aposematic animals, such as the Gila monster, are sluggish; but poison frogs are extremely active, foraging amongst the leaf litter of tropical forest where they move with short leaps. They are rarely still for more than a moment or two, so they cannot fail to attract attention.

Surprising as it may seem to some people, the majority of snakes are not venomous. Those that are dangerous to human beings are either back-fanged Colubridae, most of which chew venom into the wound caused by their bite, Elapidae, of which cobras are the most important and Viperidae. The last named family includes the subfamilies Viperinae, the true vipers and Crotalinae, the pit-vipers and rattlesnakes.

In most cases, a snake strikes rapidly in darkness and then disappears before it can be identified. The characteristic punctures made by the fangs, however, often enable diagnosis to be made. The presence of two bleeding fang marks is a clear indication that the bite is that of a dangerously poisonous species. If other tooth marks are also present, a cobra is responsible; if not, the bite will probably have been inflicted by a viper (Figure 9.4). Cobra venom acts rapidly on humans and, if death from respiratory failure does not occur within about 12 hours, the patient normally recovers quickly. In the case of viper bites, however, death is less

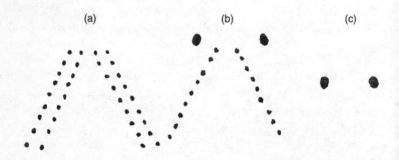

9.4 Tooth and fang marks left by: (a) Non-poisonous or mildly poisonous back-fanged snake; (b) Cobra or mamba; (c) Viper.

rapid and it may be several days before the patient is out of danger because late complications, such as haemorrhage and sepsis, are not infrequent.

No birds and, apart from shrews, few mammals are known to be venomous.

Defensive secretions

Many arthropods produce substances that render them distasteful to their enemies. In addition to the use of the poison claws in defence, centipedes produce a number of defensive secretions. Millipedes, likewise, secrete defensive secretions which are **repugnatorial** and may even cause blindness if they get into vertebrate eyes. Millipedes usually only discharge their secretion from segments that are threatened. They are thus protected from repeated attacks by small predators such as ants. Usually the repugnatorial fluids simply ooze out onto the body surface, but some large tropical species are able to eject their defensive secretions for considerable distances when attacked by vertebrates. This, however, does not prevent them from being devoured by certain enemies such as meerkats and banded mongooses.

Defensive secretions are produced by many insects and arachnids. The major invertebrate enemies of termites appear to be predatory ants. In some termite genera, the soldier caste is adapted for chemical defence. The mandibles have become atrophied and the head is drawn out into a tubular 'nose' terminating in the opening of the frontal gland from which a sticky fluid is ejected upon any attacker (Figure 9.5).

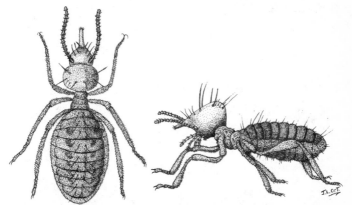

9.5   Nasute termite soldier (Nasutiterminae) seen from above and from the side (5 mm).

Beetles are prominent among the insects that are equipped with chemical defences. They include the bombardier beetles which discharge a toxic mixture at attacking predators, the chemicals reacting to produce temperatures of up to 100 °C. Most Tenebrionidae are smelly and presumably distasteful, while *Eleodes* species spray quinones in defence. Many other insects contain toxic or distasteful chemicals within their bodies. Some bleed reflexively when attacked, certain moths eject a mixture of blood and cervical gland secretions, while grasshoppers discharge their gut contents when molested. Yet other insects defaecate, while some bugs (Hemiptera) spray salivary secretions with accuracy up to 30 cm. Serious lesions may result when these contact the sensitive eyes of vertebrates.

Arachnids that produce defensive compounds *de novo* (in contrast to the sequestration of plant metabolites) include harvest spiders, whip-scorpions (Thelyphonida) and spiders of several mygalomorph families which squirt from the anus a clear liquid that may have irritating properties. Vertebrates that secrete defensive fluids include toads, snakes and mammals such as the notorious skunk.

In this chapter it has been possible to touch upon only a few of the innumerable adaptations for, and defenses against, predation that have evolved throughout the animal kingdom. No account of predation and defence would be adequate without mention of them and their ecological significance.

10 PATHOGENS, SYMBIONTS AND PARASITES

In Chapter 6, the importance of pathogens and parasites in regulating the populations of plants and animals was explained. We shall now explore the adaptations of those organisms to their ways of life, just as we did in Chapter 9 in the case of predators and their prey. There is, however, a big difference between the effects of predators and of parasites on their victims. Selection by predators on their prey results in morphological adaptations which are visible and conspicuous, whereas defences against parasites are mainly physiological and therefore not readily apparent to the ecologist.

No more intimate relationship exists between one species and another than the bond linking parasites with their hosts. Parasites have traditionally been regarded as having an impact on their host populations somewhat similar to those of predators on prey populations. Recent studies, however, indicate that the influence of parasites is much more subtle than that of predators. Parasites and pathogens may kill their hosts or have only slight, almost undetectable effects on their viability. They can alter the fecundity of the host, its competitive ability, physiology, social dominance, or its ability to attract mates. They may even be beneficial by making other intermediate hosts more readily available as prey, or by reducing the fitness of co-infested competing species.

Pathogens

Pathogens can be defined as any organisms or substances that cause **disease**; and disease is regarded as an impairment of the normal state of an organism that modifies or interrupts its vital functions. Pathogens include parasitic microorganisms such as viruses, bacteria, Protista as well as fungi and larger parasitic plants and animals. Some diseases involve both pathogens and abiotic agents in combination. Pathogens also include the enigmatic **prions** responsible for CJD in humans, scrapie in sheep and BSE among cattle.

Microparasites

Microparasites may be ecologically important in the regulation of population densities, in controlling the distribution of species, and in determining the outcome of intraspecific and interspecific competition. They reproduce directly, and usually at high rates within the host. If one bacterial cell, for instance, were to divide into two every 30 minutes, there would be a total of 8 388 608 cells within 12 hours and 16 777 216 after 12 hours 30 minutes! In contrast, macroparasites usually undergo no direct reproduction within the host. They have much longer generation times and infections by them tend to be **chronic** or persistent rather than either **transient** or, if the host succumbs, fatal. The distinction between the effects of microparasites and of macroparasites is also much more complex among animals than it is in plants.

Hosts that recover from pathogenic infections will often have developed immunity against reinfection. This is especially true among animals.

Parasites of plants

Only rod-shaped bacteria cause plant disease. They produce toxins and enzymes that destroy the tissues of their host. Bacterial diseases of plants have been studied almost entirely in relation to crop diseases. They include tobacco wilt, the blight of wheat and soy bean, the fire blight of pear and soft rot of potatoes as well as diseases of sugar cane, grapes, citrus fruits and coconuts. **Microplasms**, another group of microscopic pathogens, do not have rigid cell walls like bacteria do. They are responsible for yellows disease and are spread by insect vectors. **Viruses** which consist of DNA (deoxyribonucleic acid) or RNA (ribonucleic acid) with a protein coat, affect enzyme systems so that they are replicated over and over again. They are dispersed among plants by nematodes and insects as well as by human activities. **Viroids** are even smaller than viruses. The infective particle consists of a single strand of RNA and there is no coat of protein.

Fungi are responsible for a wide range of plant diseases. *Colletotrichum* and *Gloeosporium* fungi attack many species, particularly in humid tropical regions. The diseases for which they are responsible are known as **anthracnoses** and include leaf spot, crown rot, coffee berry disease, boll rot and the brown blight of tea. Dutch elm disease, caused by the fungus *Ceratocystis ulmi* and spread mainly by bark beetles (*Scolytus* *multistriatus*) was introduced into Europe from Asia during the First World War and killed innumerable elm trees. It reached the USA around 1930 and its effects were again disastrous.

Eelworms

Nematodes – often known as eelworms – are usually small or microscopic, slender whitish and unsegmented round-worms. They are very widely distributed and occur in large numbers, both as regards species and individuals. They are found in moist soil, water and as parasites of both plants and animals. Indeed, it was even claimed by N.A. Cobb in 1915 that, if all the matter in the universe except for nematodes were swept away, our world would still be dimly recognisable, represented by a film of nematode worms. Mountains and vales, lakes, rivers and oceans would be decipherable. The massing of human beings in towns and cities would be indicated by the corresponding massing of nematodes. In many cases, individual plants and animals could be identified by examination of their erstwhile nematode parasites.

Many species of nematodes lay their eggs in the soil and the young eelworms penetrate tender roots where their activities lead to the formation of galls. Nematodes feed by piercing plant tissues with **stylet** mouthparts. Most species feed on roots, but any part of a plant is liable to infection. Severe infestation may affect plants seriously and even lead to their death. Plant geneticists have developed many strains of domestic crops that are resistant to pathogens of various kinds, as well as to nematodes.

Parasitic plants

Almost everyone knows that mistletoes are mainly parasites of **deciduous** trees in Europe. When these have shed their leaves in winter, the common mistletoe *Viscum album* can be seen on poplars, limes, oaks and apple trees throughout Europe and northern Asia. In addition, however, another species, *V.laxum*, grows there on pines and firs while a third, *Loranthus europaeus*, lives only on oaks. Since mistletoes have green leaves and are able to photosynthesise, they are only parasitic to the extent that they absorb water and nutrients from their hosts. For this reason, they are sometimes known as **hemiparasites**.

A most remarkable feature of mistletoes is that one individual plant can live parasitically on another plant of the same species and small **superparasites** may sometimes be seen on larger mistletoes. The sticky seeds, distributed by birds that eat the fruits, germinate but do not develop roots. Instead, the young plants produce so-called **bark suckers** which penetrate the host plant and drive tapering shoots into its tissues. Mistletoes are unique among plants in that several species are mimics of their host plant. As already mentioned, a large proportion of Australian mistletoe species (excluding those of the rainforest) do so. It seems probable that the agents of selection in this case are leaf-eating possums which find mistletoes especially to their liking.

Absence of roots is characteristic of many parasitic plants. The phenomenon is also found in aquatic plants and among epiphytic bromeliads of the rainforest. Plants of the broomrape family (Orobancheae) are rootless parasites, as are silkweed plants (*Cuscuta*) which consist only of stalks and flowers. The stalks wind round their host plants from which they take all the nutrients they require through special outgrowths or **haustoria** like the bark suckers of mistletoes.

Commensalism and mutualism

Commensalism

There are many intermediate stages between a free-living existence and parasitism. One of these is **commensalism**. The term, which means 'eating at the same table', was originally given to the associations between two or more animals belonging to different species which share each other's food. Nowadays, however, it is more often extended to include benefits other than nutritional ones. For example, sea-anemones living on the shells of hermit-crabs obtain scraps from the crabs' food, while the crabs are protected by the stinging cells of the anemones. When a hermit crab which has outgrown its old shell finds a new home, it transfers the sea-anemone to it.

Another benefit sometimes derived from commensal associations is shelter from the rigours of the environment. Prawns and shrimps that live inside sponges or within the bodies of sea-cucumbers (Holothuria) provide an example, as do the many kinds of animal that live in ants' nests. In cases such as this, only one of the partners derives any benefit. Indeed, most cases of commensalism are one-sided. The **remoras** or sucker-fish that attach themselves to sharks and whales obtain protection, transport and surplus food from their hosts' meals. The latter gain nothing.

Although sharing food and the provision of shelter are the main features of commensalism, other factors also enter into some commensal associations. Moreover, since commensals are not directly dependent upon one another, they can usually survive on their own.

Many marine commensals not only derive protection from their association, but also obtain food from the currents of water conveniently produced by their hosts. Tiny pea crabs, for instance, are occasionally to be found in the tubes of fan-worms or within the shells of bivalve molluscs. Sometimes several different commensals cohabit with the same host. For instance, the burrow of a echiuroid worm often contains a scale-worm, a bivalve mollusc, a small crab and a goby fish (Figure 10.1). (The Echiuroida or 'spoon worms' is a phylum of unsegmented marine worm-like animals that feed on detritus.) Commensals that live in ant's nests, plant galls etc. and which do not benefit their hosts are known as **inquilines**.

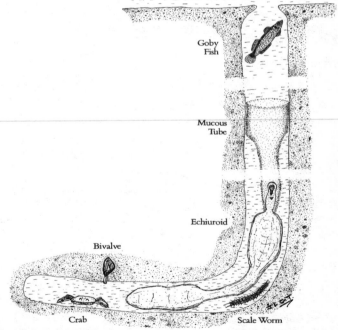

Goby Fish

Mucous Tube

Echiuroid

Bivalve

Crab

Scale Worm

10.1 Echiuroid worm in its burrow with associated commensals, all of which derive protection from sharing the burrow.

In the tropics there are many spectacular examples of birds which habitually nest close to the colonies of venomous social insects such as bees, wasps and ants. At first sight it might appear that the benefit is one-sided and that the birds obtain protection from the presence of the insects but provide nothing in return. Mutual benefit (see below) is, however, often involved. For example, in South America, yellow-backed orioles build in colonies around the nests of wasps whose presence keeps off opossums, monkeys and snakes that might otherwise eat the eggs of the orioles. To a lesser degree, however, the brightly coloured birds protect the wasps, their conspicuous yellow plumage drawing the attention of larger vertebrates to the presence of the wasps' nests that they might otherwise inadvertently damage. In Asia and Africa, too, some colourful colonial birds form similar commensal associations with social insects.

Phoresy

The meaning of **phoresy** is 'carrying'. It involves a method of dispersal in which one animal clings to the body of a larger one and is transported thereby to another place. For example, tiny false-scorpions (Pseudoscorpionida) are sometimes to be found attached to the legs of house flies; and bird-lice (Mallophaga) are frequently transported from one host to another by louse-flies (Hippoboscidae). Borborid flies (Sphaeroceridae) are often to be seen riding on the backs of scarabs and other dung-beetles in northern Africa. Although these small, black bodied flies refuse to be dislodged by any antics of the beetles, they readily evade capture, when necessary, by flight. Again, the phorid fly *Metopina pachycondylae* lives in the colonies of ponerine ants in Texas. Its small larvae cling to the necks of ant larvae by means of suckers, encircling their hosts like collars. Whenever the ant larvae are fed, the larvae of *M. pachycondylae* uncoil themselves and partake of the feast. Sometimes, when there is no food within reach, the phorid larva will tweak with its mandibles the skin of its host, or that of a neighbouring ant larva, whose wriggling then incites the worker ants to bring a fresh supply of food.

Kleptoparasitism

Some birds, notably the raptors and skuas, are **kleptoparasites** or 'pirates' and rob other birds of their food, while cuckoos and a few others are **nest parasites** or **social parasites** and lay their eggs in the nests of other species which tend and rear the parasites' young. Bees, wasps and ants which also foist their broods upon the care of others are called cuckoo-bees and so on. In contrast, **slave-making** or **dulotic** ants raid the nests of other species, removing pupae which are reared as slaves in the nests of the dulotic species and forage food for their captors.

Mutualism

The term mutualism has been defined in more ways than one. Some authorities regard it as a sub-category of **symbiosis** (see below) in which two unrelated organisms are metabolically dependent upon each other. Others use the term more generally as an association between organisms of different species from which both benefit but neither is entirely dependent on the relationship. Commensalism, mutualism, symbiosis and parasitism grade into one another and it is not possible to be more precise.

Oxpeckers perch on the backs of elephants, rhinoceroses and other African mammals where they feed upon ticks and lice. The mammals derive benefit from the association not only because they are cleansed of ectoparasites, but also because they are warned of the approach of danger when the oxpeckers fly away. The latter benefit nutritionally.

Pollination and seed dispersal by animals

So far, insects and other herbivorous animals have been considered more in relation to their harmful than to their mutualistic relationships with the vegetable kingdom. **Pollination** is one of the many inter-relationships from which both sides benefit. Pollination is the transfer of pollen from the **anthers** of one flower to the **stigmas** of another. The male sex organs or **stamens** consist of a number of anthers, in the pollen sacs of which millions of pollen grains are produced. Each grain contains and protects the male sex cell within it. The **carpel** or female sex organ contains a single ovule within its ovary. The stigma has a sticky coating to which pollen grains adhere and is connected to the ovary by a tube or **style**.

Wind pollination

Wind-pollinated flowers, such as those of grasses, willows and lime trees, pines and other conifers, are inconspicuous, usually lacking petals and the **sepals** which surround and protect these when the flowers are in bud. Wind pollination or **anemophily** has the obvious advantage to the plant of being independent of insects. On the other hand, effective wind pollination requires the production of immense quantities of pollen. It has been estimated that a single birch catkin produces about 5.5 million pollen grains and a hazel catkin about 4 million. For many plant species, mutualistic pollination by insects and other animals is evidently a highly economic alternative.

Insect pollination

It has been calculated that anemophilous plants produce more pollen than insect-pollinated plants whether pollen production is expressed in terms of stamens, flowers, inflorescences or entire plants. Nevertheless, the relationship, as in the case of so many ecological systems, is by no means clear. The genetic advantage of cross-pollination from one plant to another is indicated by the provision of a convenient place for insect pollinators to alight on and the presence of conspicuous colouring, scent and food (**nectar**) to attract them. Nectar is an aqueous, sugary solution upon which many species of butterflies, moths, wasps, bees, ants and flies depend for sustenance. Most insect-pollinated plants are adapted so that they attract specific pollinators. Those that are pollinated by nocturnal moths, for example, have flowers that are mostly white, pale rose or pale yellow in colour and are often excellent reflectors of ultraviolet light; those that are pollinated by flies during the day frequently smell of carrion or faeces.

At the same time, insect pollinators have numerous hairs to which pollen grains become attached while nectar is being gathered. Honey-bees, which feed future reproductive individuals on pollen in the form of royal jelly, have a complex apparatus consisting of hairs, rakes and 'pollen baskets' on their legs with which to gather and transport their spoils. No insect could possibly collect nectar or pollen without inadvertently transferring some of the grains from one plant to another at the same time. Some species of plants can be pollinated by several kinds of insect, but others with highly specialised pollinators have evolved structural features that not only fit them for these but exclude or discourage all others. Some flowers trap insects for a while, only releasing them after they have been covered with pollen. One of these is the wild arum or cuckoopint, the flowers of which smell of dung and attract numerous small flies. When these alight on the upper part of the **spadix** or axis of the inflorescence, they slip on its greasy surface and fall into a chamber containing nectar, which surrounds its lower part. They cannot climb out of this because they are trapped by a ring of bristles formed of sterile flowers. After a couple of days, during which pollen is shed onto them, the spadix shrinks and they are able to escape. If they are then trapped by another inflorescence on its first day, they can cause cross-pollination. On the second day, the spadix no longer produces a smell (Figure 10.2).

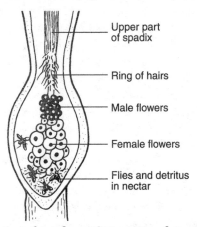

Upper part
of spadix

Ring of hairs

Male flowers

Female flowers

Flies and detritus
in nectar

10.2 Inflorescence of cuckoopint opened to show female flowers (which ripen first) at the base, male flowers and ring of hairs that prevents insects from escaping before they have fertilised the female flowers and been dusted with pollen.

Over 800 species of fig tree are found in the monsoon forests of India, each pollinated by its own species of fig wasp. The males of these tiny insects are wingless. When the females have been fertilised, they collect pollen from their own fig tree before flying to another. This they pollinate before laying their eggs in the developing fruit. Some of the wild figs are stranglers which first parasitise and then surround the host tree that originally supported them: this then dies and rots away. The twisted roots of the mature strangler form an excellent home for macaques and other species of monkey which feed on the figs and disperse their seeds (see below).

Pollination by vertebrates

Should a snail happen to creep across a plant and accidentally transfer pollen from one flower to another it could not be regarded as a true pollinator: the odds against frequent pollination in this way are far too great. True pollinators must regularly visit the plants that they pollinate. In temperate regions, where seasonal changes are pronounced, insects are the most important agents of pollination. On the other hand, in the tropics where marked seasonal variations are absent, flowering plants are often pollinated by birds and mammals. These pollinators provide a fine example of the periodism discussed in Chapter 7.

Whereas humming-birds, honey-creepers, sunbirds and lorikeets are the most important vertebrate pollinators during the hours of daylight, their place is taken at dusk by night-flying bats and certain other small mammals. For example, the baobab or tebaldi tree is occasionally pollinated by bush babies in semi-arid regions of Africa, although the normal pollinators are fruit bats. Again, the Australian marsupial honey mouse (*Tarsipes*) has become specially adapted for feeding on nectar. Its snout projects forwards and it has lost most of its teeth, but it has a very long worm-like tongue with a rough surface which is ideal for collecting nectar from the narrow tubes of flowers. Whilst doing so, pollen is unwittingly transferred from one blossom to another.

Bat pollination takes place only in the tropics. Flower-visiting bats have evolved independently in different tropical regions. In the New World, certain species whose relations are insectivorous have evolved pointed snouts and tongues for collecting nectar. In both groups the snout is long, the teeth reduced and the tongue elongated. The sonar apparatus, by which insect-eating bats detect their prey, is not well developed, but the sense of smell is unusually acute. Both nectar and pollen are eaten.

The chief characteristics of bat-pollinated flowers are that they are open from dusk to dawn. They usually have a disagreeably sour and musty scent that attracts bats and their colour is often dingy. They are strong enough to bear the weight of a bat, produce a large amount of sticky nectar and pollen and are usually exposed on bare branches and trunks. They also tend to have long, dangling stalks. These flowers are usually either bell-shaped or gullet-like in form.

Seed dispersal by animals

The principal agents for the transport of seeds are animals, wind, water and plants themselves. The resulting dispersal mechanisms are known as **zoochory**, **anemochory**, **hydrochory** and **autochory** respectively. Zoochory is an important aspect of the biotic relationship between Plantae and Animalia. The plant units that are dispersed can be simply seeds, or seeds contained within fruits, compound fruits, parts of plants or even entire plants. For the unit dispersed, R. Sernander coined the word **diaspore** (from the Greek word meaning to broadcast) in 1927. The term is used for any part of a plant, irrespective of its morphological origin. Long-distance dispersal is generally known as **telechory** while phenomena that resist telechory, wholly or partially, are collectively known as **antitelechory**, **atelechory** or **achory**. Telechory usually takes place in regions with moist climate where the vegetation forms a continuous cover and there is severe competition between plants for space and nutrients. In arid regions, where moisture is localised and plant communities usually do not have a closed canopy cover, anti-telechoretic mechanisms are more often found.

Zoochory is most important in the forest biome, but it occurs in most terrestrial environments. In the arid parts of central Australia, for example, the diaspores of 22 per cent of plant species are dispersed by animals, of which 9 per cent are ants and **myrmecochory** is widespread in dry regions. Birds cover much greater distances than mammals do and are more important agents of zoochory. External transport of diaspores by adhesion to feathers or fur is relatively unimportant compared with **endozoochory** when the diaspores are swallowed. The majority of zoochorous seeds are embedded in succulent fruits. When these are eaten the seeds are not digested but are voided, often far from where the fruits were originally found.

Some seeds actually require the stimulus of passing through the alimentary canal of a bird or mammal before they will germinate: others are digested or harmed by this. In the past, the poisons produced by plants were regarded only as anti-herbivory agents. It is now recognised, however, that fruit purgatives such as those found in the pods of *Cassia senna* cause seeds to be voided rapidly which enhances their chances of germination. The fruits of zoochorotic seeds are usually brightly coloured and thereby attract the birds, mammals or reptiles that feed on them.

Symbiosis

Dissimilar organisms that spend a part of their lives very intimately associated with other organisms of a different species are known as **symbionts** and the relationship is called **symbiosis** which, from its Greek origin, means 'living together'. As originally defined, this term embraced all types of parasitic or mutualistic relationships but in modern usage it is usually restricted to mutually beneficial interactions.

A classical example of mutualistic symbiosis is provided by the lichens. These complex organisms consist of fungi in symbiotic association with algae. They are therefore combinations of members of two different kingdoms. The fungi benefit nutritionally from the photosynthesising algal cells, while the latter derive shelter and protection from the fungi. The word symbiosis was first coined in 1879 by the German botanist Heinrich A. De Bary to describe this particular relationship. Lichens can survive in extreme environments where neither of the symbionts apparently exists on its own.

Many of the symbiotic relationships involving microorganisms and other life forms are largely dependent upon nitrition. The root nodule bacteria of leguminous plants have already been mentioned in respect of the part they play in the nitrogen cycle. Many trees and other plants have fungal threads or **mycelia** growing in and around their roots and forming complexes known as **mycorrhizas**. The fungi assimilate nutritients from the soil, some of which are passed on to the plants. Some of the tropical orchids that lack chlorophyll are able to live saprophytically thanks to mycorrhizas that break down organic material for them. (**Saprophytes** and **saprozoites**, it will be remembered, are organisms that absorb soluble organic nutrients from non-living sources such as dead plant or animal matter and dung.)

Nutrition-dependent symbioses between invertebrate animals and microorganisms have also been recognised. Corals (Chapter 5) provide a well-known example. They are colonial Cnidaria with calcareous exoskeletons. Like those of their relatives, the sea anemones, the polyps of corals possess tentacles with stinging cells by which food is captured while, embedded in their tissues, are unicellular algae known collectively as **zooxanthellae**. The latter obtain protection from the polyps and utilise some of their waste products. In return, they release oxygen that the polyps can use and some of them may also be digested by the polyps. The brilliant colours of most shallow water corals are due to the presence of these flagellated Protista.

The ship-worm, a marine mollusc that burrows into wood, has a gut flora containing bacteria that digest cellulose and lignin, the principal structural materials of plants. Many insects possess special cells known as **mycetocytes** containing bacteria and yeasts which produce the vitamins and other growth factors needed by their hosts.

The best-known example of symbiosis amongst vertebrates is provided by cattle and other mammals that chew the cud. These have a stomach characterised by three or four parts one of which, the **rumen**, contains millions of symbiotic bacteria and other microorganisms that produce the enzyme **cellulase**. This breaks down the **cellulose** in the food of their mammalian hosts so that it can be digested. Termites are able to digest cellulose with the aid, not of bacteria but of symbiotic Protista that inhabit a fermentation chamber in the hind-gut. Without these symbionts within them, the termites would die. All insects that feed upon wood appear to be dependent upon symbiotic microorganisms or fungi so that they can digest both the cellulose and lignin of which wood is composed.

Parasitism among animals

No form of association is ecologically more important than parasitism, the ecological significance of which has already been outlined. Parasitism is an extremely diverse and varied phenomenon. It may be obvious that a tape-worm or a louse is parasitic, but what of a leech which may kill and eat its victim outright, or merely suck a little blood? Many parasites are **obligate** and, for part of their lives at least, are unable to exist away from a host. Others, known as **facultative** parasites, may be entirely free living, but adopt a parasitic mode of life when the opportunity arises. In fact, there are all degrees of association from a free-living existence to being completely dependent upon a host organism. This adds to the difficulty of classifying categories that grade into one another.

Parasites can also be roughly divided into ectoparasites and endoparasites, but this arrangement is rather artificial because innumerable intermediate stages exist. Furthermore, the attentions of ectoparasites may cause reactions in the internal organisms of the host. Nevertheless, true ectoparasites show different adaptations for their ways of life than do endoparasites. Extremes are easy to distinguish; it is the 'grey' areas between them that cause problems of classification.

Ectoparasitism

Varying degrees of ectoparasitism are apparent in the animal kingdom. Some ectoparasites, such as mosquitoes and bed bugs, lampreys, hagfish and vampire bats, are **intermittent** parasites and visit their hosts only occasionally and long enough to obtain a meal of blood; while others, such as lice may leave their host only when moulting or mating takes place. Some ticks of the family Ixodidae never leave their host until the final egg-laying excursion from which there is no return.

Ectoparasitic arthropods show a number of characteristic features. They usually have flattened bodies and strong claws for holding on to the hairs of their hosts. A leathery integument helps them to withstand rough treatment from their host in the form of scratching and squeezing. Sense organs tend to be reduced, wings lost and legs adapted for slow crawling. To the inexperienced eye, a louse-fly (Diptera Hippoboscidae) looks very much like a true louse (Anoplura), a bed bug (Hemiptera Heteroptera) or even a tick (Arachnida: Ixodidae). This is a fine example of convergence (Figure 10.3).

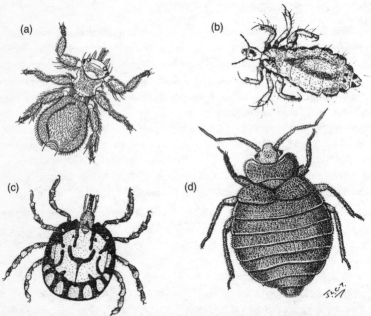

10.3 Ectoparasitic arthropods: (a) Louse-fly; (b) Louse; (c) Tick; (d) Bed bug. (Not to scale.)

Fleas are somewhat different in appearance and only the adults are parasitic. These have a tough cuticle and are difficult to squash, but they are flattened laterally instead of dorso-ventrally. In addition, they have well-developed powers of locomotion and, it seems, are adapted for moving rapidly through short, dense fur whilst lice crawl among coarser, long hairs. If a flea were to be compared with an antelope living in open, grassy savanna, a louse would have to be likened to a chimpanzee swinging among the branches of the forest.

Some ectoparasites, such as leeches and ticks, frequently endure long fasts between meals. Their alimentary canals are extended into pouches in which the blood they have eaten is stored and from which it can be slowly absorbed, Nearly all blood-sucking animals – leeches, worms, insects, ticks, mites and vampire bats – have developed an enzyme in their saliva which prevents coagulation of the host's blood during feeding. With such saliva into the host's body, many endoparasites such as Protista and Nematoda are also introduced. Chigoes or jiggers (*Tunga penetrans*) are the most completely parasitic of the fleas (Figure 10.4). The males and immature females spend most of the time in dry, dusty soil, but mature females burrow into the skin of the feet of human beings, pigs and other large mammals. The tip of the flea's abdomen remains just outside the surface, ejecting the eggs which fall to the ground. When the embedded female eventually dies, her body remains under the skin, often causing inflammation and ulceration.

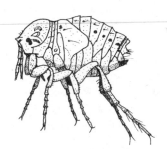 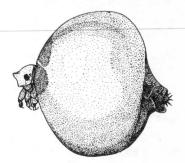

10.4 Chigoe (*Tunga penetrans*). Immature and gravid females. (Not to scale.)

Ectoparasites provide magnificent examples of morphological adaptation to the environment – the exterior of the body of another animal. The responses of the host to such parasitism are less dramatic. They consist chiefly in physiological tolerance of bites and in scratching, grooming and toilet behaviour. Mutual grooming plays an important part in the daily life of most social animals. Indeed, it would be interesting to know to what extent ectoparasites and the resulting grooming have contributed to the evolution of social behaviour among mammals.

Endoparasitism

Endoparasites are ecologically far more significant than ectoparasites except when the latter act as the **intermediate** hosts that transit them to new hosts. The most important endoparasites of animals are viruses, bacteria, Protista and 'worms' belonging to the phyla Platyhelminthes and Nematoda. The Platyhelminthes include parasitic flukes and the tape-worms, whilst the Nematoda comprise various hook-worms, intestinal round-worms and the filarial worms responsible for human diseases such as elephantiasis and onchocerciasis. The chief protistan parasites are the dysentery amoebas, trypanosomes which cause human sleeping-sickness and 'nagana' of cattle, as well as the spirochaetes responsible for relapsing fever, syphilis and yaws.

Endoparasites are almost invariably far more closely dependent upon their hosts than are ectoparasites. Protected by the bodies of these hosts and surrounded by an abundance of food, many of them are saprozoitic and there is often no need for digestive systems, locomotory mechanisms, or sense-organs. The consequent simplifications of structure are sometimes erroneously thought to be 'degenerate'.

Many internal parasites absorb food through the surface of the body and there is a tendency for their mouths and digestive organs to become atrophied. Helminth parasites, however, often have adhesive organs such as hooks and suckers by which they maintain a hold inside the alimentary canal of their host. Tape-worms secrete anti-enzymes which neutralise the digestive enzymes of the host and, like round-worms, have tough cuticles which are resistent to digestion.

The security offered by the body of a host improves the chances of a parasite's survival. The major hazards in its life-cycle occur in finding a new host: correlated with this, parasitic animals are extremely prolific. A human tape-worm, for example, may live for 10 to 20 years, every month budding off several ripe segments or **proglottids**, each of which is loaded with thousands of eggs. Blood-flukes of the genus *Schistosoma*, which cause bilharzia, can live in human beings for up to 40 years and produce a very large number of eggs during this time. These eggs develop in water to form **miracidium** larvae which infect the second host, a species of snail. Several generations of **sporocyst** and **redia** larvae, formed asexually, are passed within the body of the snail before the final appearance of the **cercariae** which reinfect people. A snail infected by a single miracidium has been known to discharge over 200 000 cercariae at a rate of 3500 per day.

A single round-worm (*Ascaris lumbricoides*) can produce 200 000 microscopic eggs a day and it has been estimated that one female may contain as many as 27 million eggs. In China, some years ago, American observers found that about 335 million people were infected. They estimated that the weight of eggs produced each year inside these people would amount to 18 000 tonnes! These figures give an idea of the tremendous mortality that must be experienced by the development stages of such parasites. Moreover, the presence of both sexual and asexual generations in the life-cycles of many species greatly increases the fecundity of most animal parasites.

Not only do parasites have to find a suitable host but there is a further difficulty in finding a sexual partner after a host has been obtained. For this reason, the males and females of many blood-flukes live in permanent union. In some cases the male is dwarfed and permanently attached to the female. In one species of round-worm, the male actually lives as a parasite inside the vagina of the female. Another solution to the problem frequently resorted to is **parthenogenesis** or the development of unfertilised eggs. This is a dangerous procedure, however, for asexual reproduction reduces the viability of the species concerned.

The ways in which endoparasites can enter the body of a new host are limited. A few, like the cercariae of *Schistosoma* bore through the skin or enter natural openings leading into the ducts of the respiratory, urinary or genital organs. Parasites hardly ever enter a host through its anus: the majority are ingested with food or injected by the bites of blood-sucking arthropods. For this reason the simplest control measures usually consist in the avoidance of infection by destruction of the invertebrate hosts – snails, mosquitoes, black-flies, tsetse flies, sand-flies, lice, fleas, mites, ticks and so on, as well as of the house-flies that merely carry parasites to human food.

Many parasites such as flukes, tape-worms, filarial worms and malarial parasites have two-host life-cycles. In most cases the secondary host is a blood-sucking insect but, in tape-worms, it is a pig or cow. Some parasites may have three or four intermediate hosts: these include flukes whose life-cycles pass through humans to aquatic snails, thence to fish and back to humans when the fish is eaten.

Parasitic life-cycles are often extremely complicated. The best known is probably that of the malarial parasite (*Plasmodium*), illustrated in Figure 10.5. In 1897, Ronald Ross, an army doctor in India, discovered that malaria is transmitted by the bites of *Anopheles* mosquitoes. The parasites are injected into the human bloodstream along with the saliva of the mosquito. Each of them enters a liver cell where it feeds at the expense of its host. When full grown, some of these parasites return to the blood and invade the red cells.

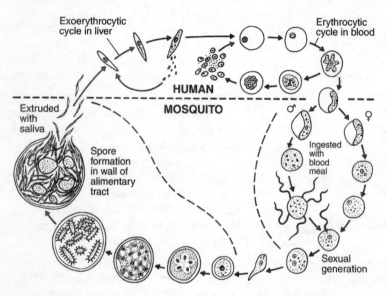

10.5 Life-cycle of the malarial parasite (*Plasmodium*).

When another mosquito bites a human infected with malaria, parasites are taken up with its blood meal. They pass through a sexual generation with males and female cells before forming cysts on the wall of the mosquito's alimentary or food canal. Here spore formation takes place and the spores move into the saliva of the mosquito, ready to infect another person next time the mosquito takes a meal. Malaria is transmitted by infected female mosquitoes only, because males do not suck blood.

Parasitoids

Unlike parasites, parasitoids are relatively large in size when compared with their hosts and this is mainly responsible for their fatal consequences. Although most examples, such as ichneumons, attack arthropods, a few parasitise other invertebrates. The larvae of the cluster-fly *Pollenia rudis*, for example, are parasitoids of the common European earthworm *Allolobophora chlorotica*. The female fly deposits her eggs in the soil during the autumn and, on hatching, the larvae penetrate by way of the male genital openings into the body cavities and sperm-sacs of earthworms. During the following winter the larva does not feed but, when the temperature of the soil rises in spring, it migrates forwards until it reaches the anterior end of its host where it penetrates the skin and protrudes its post-abdominal spiracles. It now begins to feed actively, growing quickly as it devours the tissues of its host. Eventually the worm is almost entirely consumed and the fly larva buries itself in the soil where it forms a **puparium** from which an adult fly emerges. The larva of a related fly is parasitic on snails, where it develops in the kidney. Later, all the organs of the host are attacked in turn and the snail dies before the larva is full grown. The parasitoid then becomes saprophagous, living upon the decomposing remains of the snail. When its food is exhausted, it leaves the now empty shell of its dead host and pupates underground.

Evolution of parasitism

A parasite is an organism which, during some stage of its life, is not only in intimate association with an individual of another species but is, to some degree, dependent upon it metabolically. Parasitism is, therefore, a relative phenomenon and it should be possible to draw up a list of parasitic species showing an increasing degree of metabolic dependence on their hosts. Between the extremes of free-living animals and total parasites are numerous organisms which satisfy their metabolic requirements to a varying extent at the expense of the host.

The ectoparasitic habit in arthropods probably arose from the intermittent sucking of blood by free-living species and, in its most primitive form, cannot be distinguished from the behaviour of predatory animals that suck the body juices from prey smaller than themselves. Indeed, the chief difference is one of size: the more predatory type of feeding utilises small prey while blood-sucking parasites attack larger animals which are not usually killed. Tsetse flies are evolutionarily well on the way to becoming true ectoparasites like their relations, the louse-flies. As a result of competition for living space, an ectoparasite may sometimes creep into some convenient orifice of its host's body. This is the first step towards endoparasitism. Thus one species of black-fly, of which the males are not parasitic at all, mates in the ears of the female's host. In due course, both sexes may develop endoparasitic habits. If a leech crawls up the anus of a hippopotamus or into the trunk of an elephant and there finds an abundance of food, it has already graduated to the rank of endoparasite.

Many flies, although normally breeding in decaying vegetation and dead carcasses, will occasionally deposit their eggs in the diseased tissues of human beings and other animals. Oviposition is stimulated by foul and fetid odours and these flies will not deposit eggs or larvae on clean wounds or unbroken skin. Fly maggots are well able to live parasitically in the pus of septic wounds and sores where they may cause severe lesions, as in the case of sheep 'strike'. On the other hand, when sterile, they have been used to clean infected wounds, since they normally feed on diseased rather than healthy tissue. Ectoparasitism often arises from the blood-sucking habit and from this may develop into endoparasitism. By no means all internal parasites have passed through an ectoparasitic or predatory stage, however. Commensalism and accidental introductions may equally well develop into parasitism. The parasitic mode of life can develop quickly or slowly: it can arise from blood-sucking or from scavenging. It is but a short step from a dead to a living animal and scavenging animals which occasionally try blood as an alternative meal are following one of the well-trodden evolutionary paths to parasitism (Figure 10.6).

As the relationship between parasite and host becomes closer, facultative parasites become obligate and the phenomena of disease and tolerance grow in importance. Indeed, it is quite probable that symbiosis may result from mutual tolerance and adaptation carried to the furthest extreme, so that organisms, originally in conflict, have finally become indispensable allies. The better that a parasite is adapted, the less damage will it cause to its host.

Effects on the host

The harm that is caused by parasites depends very largely on their numbers and on the otherwise healthy state of the host. A diet containing

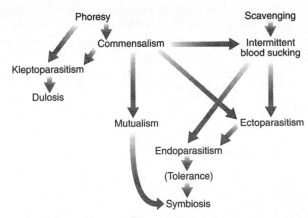

10.6 Evolutionary interactions between various types of animal association.

adequate protein is necessary for the production of antibodies. The poorer the diet, the more severe the infection must become before protein is diverted to antibody production. Some individual animals and humans possess a natural hereditary resistance to particular parasites and recovery from a disease usually confers immunity for varying periods of time. Resistance to infectious diseases increases with age, often resulting from acquired immunity. Some parasites are held in check by the defences of the host, without being completely eliminated, so that a quiescent state is sometimes reached, as in syphilis and malaria among human beings. Any lowering of the resistance of the host, resulting from genetic or environmental factors, undernourishment or some other infection, upsets this delicate balance and symptoms of the disease return. Thus, manifestations of disease can often be regarded as a sign of temporary setback in the conflict between the host animal and its parasites. Even if the disease is not serious, it may make the host less cautious than usual and therefore more likely to be killed by a predator.

11 | BIOMASS, BIODIVERSITY AND HUMAN INFLUENCES ON THE ENVIRONMENT

Since life originated, nearly 4 000 000 000 years ago, there have been continual evolutionary developments among living organisms. These developments have been in response, not only to climatic and geological changes, but also to natural selection by biotic factors. Such developments have not necessarily been cumulative, sequential or confined to a single lineage of plants or animals; they have shown a tendency towards increasing morphological and physiological complexity and sophistication. At the same time, the ecosystems of the world have also evolved and changed. Like the changes in living organisms, some of those reflected in the evolution of habitats have been slow and gradual, others sudden and comparatively abrupt.

Until its final throes at the K–T (Cretaceous–Tertiary) boundary when the dinosaurs and other giant reptiles became extinct, the Cretaceous period was a time of warm, comparatively stable climate and of **stasis** or very gradual evolutionary change. The chalk measures were deposited with minor variations in their composition, while gradually increasing complexity appeared in the shells of the marine ammonoids and nautiloids – primitive squid-like cephalopods with beautiful internal structured shells which are incorporated among those of the foraminiferidans. At the end of the Cretaceous all this changed. The world experienced first the onset of a variable climate and later a series of glacial periods interspersed by warmer ones. Each of these changes has been recorded by corresponding changes in the fossil record. Ice ages are due to a combination of numerous physical factors and no single hypothesis is adequate to explain the cause of glaciation. The most important factor, however, is a reduction in the amount of solar energy falling on the Earth, according to the Yugoslav physicist M. Milankovitch who investigated the subject in 1930.

There have been five major mass extinctions since the Palaeozoic era, in addition to several lesser ones. All of them were caused by climatic changes sometimes associated with continental movements resulting from plate tectonics. In addition, changes in sea level, volcanism, impacts with bolides and other physical causes may have been implicated. The major extinctions occurred at the close of the Ordovician, Devonian, Permian, Triassic and Cretaceous periods, when the numbers of families of marine invertebrates declined by 12, 14, 52, 12 and 11 per cent respectively. The extinction at the end of the Permian was by far the most severe. (The world total of extinction of families is shown in Appendix IV.)

These extinctions were all due to environmental effects. The sixth and latest, which began some 10 000 years ago, is unique in being caused by the destructive influence of a single species, *Homo sapiens*, whose numbers have reached plague proportions. There is no ecosystem on Earth that has not been affected in some way or another by human activities, but it is often difficult to distinguish between those changes that have been induced by humankind and those which are the result of natural causes. A good example is afforded by the current uncertainty over global warming (see below).

Biomass and biological diversity

In 1758, Linnaeus listed about 9000 species of animals. Today nearly 5 million have been described, although perhaps as many as 30 to 40 per cent of them may be **synonyms** – that is, different names given to the same species. New species are continually being recognised, however, and guesses as to the total number in existence vary from 3 to 30 million. Most of these are insects living in the canopy of the tropical rainforest – which is being destroyed by humankind at an alarming rate. Indeed, habitat destruction, mainly in the tropics, is probably driving thousands of species to extinction every year. The consequences may be dire for the human species because the flora and fauna of the rainforest is the most important and least utilised of natural resources and a gene pool awaiting investigation.

If the vast population of human beings alive today is to continue expanding, or even achieve stability, new food crops will be required to support it. At the same time, with the rapid world-wide spread of diseases

– for which air travel is largely responsible – new epidemics will continue to appear. To combat them, new drugs, as yet undiscovered, will be necessary. The risk of population crashes for whatever reason is greatly increased when ecological systems are simplified and the vast biomass of a smaller number of species replaces the smaller biomasses of a much larger number of species.

Human influences on the environment

Human beings affect the environment in countless different ways. Only a few examples, however, can be mentioned in a single book.

Human control of productivity

Control of plant and herbivore productivity by people engaged in agriculture and pastoralism has influenced terrestrial ecosystems increasingly during the past 10 000 years. Up to 15 per cent of the total land surface of the Earth is now devoted to agriculture and little remains where the soils and climates are suitable for high biological productivity. Agricultural ecosystems are to be found on all the continents except Antarctica and the ways in which human food production affects terrestrial ecosystems vary from one region to another. Nevertheless, the number of species of plants and animals involved is small. For instance, only eight species of grain are cultivated world-wide. Whereas natural ecosystems contain numerous species of plants, herbivores and carnivores, human-dominated ecosystems contain few plant species, even fewer herbivores and a single dominant omnivore, *Homo sapiens*. It is through the ability to exploit both small grain and large mammalian herbivores as food that humankind has been able to become so numerous.

Environmental exploitation

Recent expansion of the human population has only been possible because agricultural productivity has increased. But this has not been achieved without cost to the environment. Genetic research has created **miracle rice** and other crops that produce heavy yields. These, however, require a great deal more fertiliser than their predecessors did, and these fertilisers are pollutants. In addition, they kill the fishes that used to add a valuable source of protein to the diet of the people who grow the rice.

Desertification

Most of the environmental degradation that is taking place throughout arid regions of the world today is the consequence of overgrazing by domesticated animals, felling of trees for fuel by impoverished pastoralists and farmers, and over-cultivation. It has been said that the desert is the cradle of civilisation: certainly, throughout their existence, civilised people have been turning their birthplace into a desert. On a world-wide scale, deserts are probably expanding faster now than ever before in the history of humanity – faster even than they did between 1914 and 1934 which was a period during which more soil was lost to the world through erosion than had previously been lost in the whole of human history. That was the time when the dust-bowl of North America was created. The topsoil, lacking cohesion after ploughing and the natural grass cover being replaced by wheat, blew away and the land became desert. Much of this desert was later recovered, but only at considerable cost.

Wherever land is cheap, there is inevitable pressure to graze cattle – although the meat produced may still be far too expensive for the poverty-stricken local peasantry to be able to afford to buy it. In Central and South America, for instance, after valuable hardwoods have been exploited by the logging companies, often at great cost to the remainder of the forest, land-starved peasants move in and plant subsistence crops with, perhaps, some cash-crops such as coffee, chillies, cocoa and bananas. When the cleared land has lost most of its fertility, large corporations buy it up very cheaply, sow fast-growing grasses and ranch cattle at densities as low as one animal per hectare. The lean beef thus produced is ideal for making hamburgers at extremely competitive prices, but the soil becomes completely devastated and is reduced to desert after as little as 15 years.

Overproduction of cash-crops, especially groundnuts, has seriously reduced the fertility of the soil in many arid and semi-arid countries of the world. Fallow periods are reduced and poor peasant farmers are compelled to encroach on land upon which the pastoral nomads depend for grazing their stock. They are therefore compelled to keep their cattle throughout the year in dry savanna land which previously had only been used in the rainy season. Consequently, there is no reserve to fall back on during inevitable periods of drought. So the cattle die and the population is reduced to starvation. Large-scale schemes to prevent this are fraught with disaster. More agricultural land is currently being lost through salinisation and waterlogging than is being created by new irrigation schemes.

Introduced domesticated animals that escaped and became **feral** are responsible for the extermination of innumerable **endemic** species, especially on oceanic islands. (An endemic species is one that is restricted to one particular region and is found nowhere else.) Moreover, some introduced species such as goats – and rabbits in Australia – have caused severe environmental degradation. The unwise introduction of exotic species is one of the major ways in which biodiversity has been reduced.

Threats to the biosphere

Global warming and atmospheric pollution

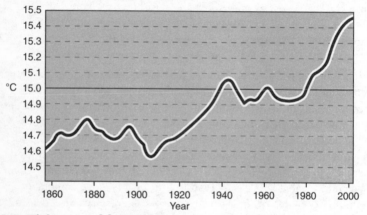

11.1 Rising world temperatures.

It is usually accepted that the world temperature is rising and this assumption is supported by graphs such as that shown in Figure 11.1, which indicates a rise of nearly 1 °C in less than a century. The question that immediately springs to mind is, where were these temperatures measured? Most meteorological stations are situated near large towns, often at airports. Are the measurements made there representative of what is happening throughout the entire world? Probably so, but one cannot be sure. There is much debate on the subject. Indeed, a respectable body of opinion even argues that increases in atmospheric carbon dioxide are the consequences of global warming – if that is really taking place – and not its cause. Industrial production of greenhouse gases is trivial compared with the amounts absorbed by the plankton of the oceans.

The Pleistocene epoch, which began approximately 2 million years ago, was marked in the northern hemisphere by several glacial and interglacial phases. The last of the ice ages ended some 10 000 years ago. Changes from cold to warm phases may, in the past, have taken only a few thousand years but changes from warm to cold have been much slower, averaging about 100 000 years. Summer insolation is believed to have decreased sharply during the last 9000 years and, apart from human influences, a gradual reduction in world temperatures might well be expected to occur during the next 50 000 years. On the other hand, if the human-induced 'greenhouse effect' manifests itself in the manner that is often forecast, global warming will take place very much faster and temperatures could well reach higher levels than they did in any of the post-Pleistocene interglacial phases.

Climatic warming due to increased carbon dioxide in the atmosphere, generally believed to be the result of excessive burning of fossil fuels including petroleum, concurrently with the felling of tropical rainforest, was mentioned in Chapter 3. One aspect of climatic change due to the greenhouse effect thereby engendered appears to be increased frequency of **El Niño**. This oceanic event causes drought in South East Asia and Australia, floods in the western parts of South America, especially Peru, and other changes unfavourable to the continued existence of human civilisation in its present form.

In normal times, the warm waters of the western Pacific are trapped in place by the trade winds blowing from the south-east. When these winds fail, in El Niño years, the warm waters flow eastward towards Equador and Peru. The fishing industry (which is ultimately dependent upon phosphates and other nutrients brought from Antarctic waters by the cold Humboldt current) collapses, the ecosystem of the Galapagos Islands is altered and there are floods in the Andes.

Flames began raging across Indonesia in July 1997, but the fires had actually begun some years earlier. They were started by human beings clearing the forest, but got completely out of control because, thanks to El Niño, the monsoon failed. Dense smog and pollution blanketed much of south-east Asia including Malaya, Borneo, New Guinea, Java and Sumatra. A number of forest ecosystems, including heath and peat swamp forests were threatened and the special soil conditions required for their regeneration have been destroyed. Coral reefs and mangroves were put at risk by increased run-off and erosion resulting from the removal of the forest. There have also been huge fires in South America.

It is quite impossible accurately to forecast any aspect of the future. The only thing one can almost be sure of is that events will not turn out as expected. A decade or so ago, many scientists were prophesying 'nuclear winter' in the aftermath of atomic warfare. The threat today is of global warming, the outcome of which cannot be predicted with certainty. The range and activity of the monsoon might well increase – as it has in past shifts from cold to warm phases. The Sahara would then invade southern Europe while Sahelian vegetation with its associated fauna would extend into regions that are currently extreme desert. Increased evaporation from the oceans would result in heavier rainfall in some places, but make the problem of desertification (see above) even worse than it is at present. Melting of the ice caps could well result in extensive flooding of low-lying regions of the globe. It is not impossible, however, that increased snowfall over the ice caps could result in their expansion and a fall in the sea level!

Concurrently with rising concentrations of carbon dioxide, other atmospheric pollutants, including chlorofluorocarbon and nitrous oxide emissions, are destroying the ozone layer of the atmosphere. The immediate effects of this are likely to include increased incidence of skin cancer among human beings, as well as more extensive damage to many other species of animals and plants, including food crops. There is sufficient space to give no more than a couple of examples.

The population of krill, upon which baleen whales, crab-eating seals and many other secondary and tertiary consumers are ultimately dependent, may be suffering from a combination of the effects of ozone depletion, global warming and over-fishing, thereby causing major disruptions in Antarctic food chains. Thinning of the ozone layer over that part of the world has lead to increasing exposure to UVB, further exacerbated by the reduction in ice cover due to global warming. This, in turn, has caused a decline in the phytoplankton upon which krill feed and may even kill krill larvae directly.

Many amphibians, particularly frogs and toads, are declining rapidly in numbers throughout the world and several species have become extinct in recent years. While most of these catastrophes are probably due to habitat destruction, some species have declined in national parks and other areas set aside for the protection of diversity. Several possible causes have been suggested, including various aspects of climatic change, especially increased levels of UVB light, due to the ozone gap and to many other consequences of pollution. In Central America, many frogs are killed by a disease (caused by protistan parasites) the symptoms of which include thickening of the skin so that cutaneous respiration cannot take place. A similar disease is apparently responsible for the mass deaths of frogs in Queensland, Australia. Ecologists believe that natural disasters such as these are the results of complex causes. Pollutants become dispersed world-wide, enter food webs and render living organisms more susceptible to disease than they would otherwise be.

Pollution at ground level

The effects of pollution at ground level are apparent everywhere, both on land and at sea. They are one of the major causes of the loss of biodiversity which characterises the present wave of extinction. Pollution is a by-product of human activities and pollutants are the residues of discarded artefacts – the concomitants of advanced technology. They include glass and plastic, the spoil from mines, pesticides and herbicides, industrial discharges, nuclear waste, exhaust gases from internal combustion engines and the emissions from power stations. These are partly responsible for acid rain and global warming. Pollutants are increasing, both because of population increase and as a result of higher living standards. Although the extent of pollution is greatest in the industrial countries of the world, many of the products manufactured by them are exported to the developing countries whose economy is primarily based on agriculture.

Freshwater lakes, such as the Great Lakes of North America (which are the world's greatest reservoir of fresh water), suffer from eutrophication resulting from the discharge into them of chemical nutrient wastes. Marine pollution damages the plankton of the oceans, while discarded plastic bags kill turtles which eat them, mistaking them for jelly-fishes; crude oil discharges are lethal to shore life and so on. The list is endless.

The increased human population has innumerable side effects. Each day, it is said, some 3500 tonnes of dog manure are deposited in the streets of New York, Chicago, Los Angeles and the other great cities of the United States of America. Each day, these same streets are sprayed with some 45 million litres of urine! At the same time, in other parts of the world, people are diseased, malnourished or starving.

Some chemical wastes harm the world's fauna by operating like female sex hormones. In consequence, male animals tend to become less fertile, sex ratios are upset and populations decline. This effect is apparent in many groups of animals including fishes and amphibians. In some of Britain's rivers and streams, for example, male fishes exposed to factory waste and treated sewage become infertile, **hermaphrodite** and possessing both testes and ovaries, or else change sex completely. The same pollutants could be responsible for falling sperm counts amongst human beings and other mammals.

The eggs of birds – especially those of predatory **raptors** at the apex of food chains where DDT accumulates – develop thin shells and fail to hatch. For this reason, the use of DDT has largely been discontinued. Ecological knowledge is helping to pinpoint many of the major dangers of pollution and some of the worst cases occurred before this knowledge was available. Nevertheless, this is no time for world governments to cut expenditure on ecological research, or on the museums and universities in which essential taxonomy is carried out.

Regulation of the human population

In Chapter 6 it was explained how experimental animal populations increase either logarithmically until they reach an asymptote (S-shaped curve) or crash catastrophically (J-shaped curve). Where only a single species is concerned, the asymptote is controlled, or the crash is caused either by shortage of food, conditioning of the environment or by density effects. In nature, growth curves are smoothed and regulated by abiotic factors as well as by the interaction of predators and parasites with their prey or hosts respectively.

Whereas animal populations are thus limited mainly by death rates, populations of human beings in developed countries tend to be influenced almost entirely by their birth rates. Even in the poorer developing countries, the human population is still increasing rapidly, despite famine, disease and density effects. A glance at a graph of the world population (Figure 11.2) shows instantly that continued increase at the present rate is impossible, as emphasised earlier.

The ability of the world to produce ever-increasing food and other resources is not unlimited. The enormous growth in productivity that has been achieved since the 1940s has failed to catch up with the population explosion and an unacceptably large proportion of humanity is doomed to a life of hunger, squalor and disease. Inevitably, the human population

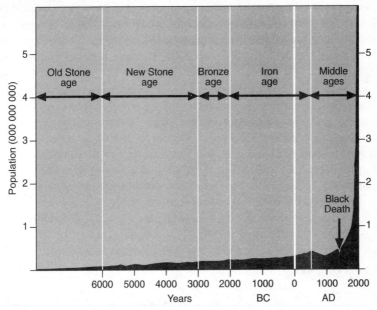

11.2 The human population of the world.

curve will reach an asymptote or there will be a crash. The possible limiting factors would appear to be one or more of the following:

1 Food shortages and starvation;
2 Warfare and weapons of mass destruction;
3 Disease;
4 Contraception and family planning world-wide.

Only the last can hope to regulate human populations without causing intense suffering, but none of the other possibilities can be excluded.

Some authorities have estimated that the human population curve will level out and reach an asymptote of about 11 to 12 000 000 000 people by the middle of the twenty-first century. This is because birth rate almost invariably drops as living standards improve and more people practice contraception. It is assumed, probably correctly, that food production per unit area will continue to increase with genetically improved crops and greater use of artificial fertilisers. But this cannot take place without increased pollution, unless ecological problems rather than commercial profits are the issues addressed first. And this will have to be achieved despite an almost inevitable decline in living standards in more technically advanced countries until the mid twenty-first century.

The environmental movement and conservation

The environmental movement has achieved some spectacular successes which give hope for the preservation of some of the world's biodiversity. Unfortunately, by appealing to the prejudices of the public without first carefully considering the scientific evidence, considerable harm has also probably been done. To give one example, public pressure has been aroused to prevent the dumping of waste in the depths of the ocean before tests could be carried out to determine whether this would indeed be environmentally harmful. Of course, it would be better to have less waste – better too, to have a smaller world population – but, if it is accepted that some waste is inevitable, it is probably less harmful at the bottom of the sea than in land fills or burned so that it pollutes the atmosphere.

Conserving biodiversity and genetic variation can be extremely expensive. For instance, preservation of the northern spotted owl cost US $9.7 million, the grizzly bear US $5.9 million, the ocelot US $3.0 million, the valley elderberry longhorn beetle US $925 000 and the northern wild monkshood US $226 000. Sums of this kind do not escape from being questioned, and criteria for the selection of species and of biotic communities for conservation need to be evaluated on the basis of ecological rather than for commercial or political reasons. It is quite impossible to conserve every species of plant and animal in imminent danger of extinction. Choices have to be made between all deserving species, not merely the high profile birds, mammals and selected plants. Ecological knowledge is essential if correct decisions are to be made for the future of humanity and the entire planet on which we live.

APPENDIX I

Classification of living organisms

Although several different classifications exist, living organisms are often divided into five kingdoms as follows:

1 **Monera**. (Bacteria and Cyanobacteria or blue-green algae, which consist of single cells without a nucleus.)

2 **Protista**. (Single-celled organisms with a nucleus: also organisms, like algae, which may be composed of filaments of cells.)

3 **Plantae**. (Plants. These obtain energy from sunlight and, with the aid of the green pigment chlorophyll, photosynthesise carbohydrates from carbon dioxide and water.)

4 **Fungi**. (Single-celled and multicellular yeasts, slime moulds, toadstools and mushrooms. They lack the chlorophyll which enables plants to synthesise carbohydrates with the aid of sunlight. Instead, they obtain energy by decomposing organic matter from decaying, and sometimes living, plants and animals.)

5 **Animalia**. (Multicellular animals such as sponges, insects, fish, frogs, snakes, birds and mammals.)

Many of the Protista (Protozoa) are also regarded as animals, for classification is not precise and is often a matter of convenience. An example of the way in which classification is inevitably inexact is afforded by the slime moulds, classified above as Fungi (Myxomycetes) (Figure A1). On account of their resemblance to colonial amoebae (Rhizopoda) they can equally well be grouped with the latter among protozoans as Mycetozoida in the kingdom Animalia. If, however, protozoans are classified as a separate kingdom (Protista), the slime moulds could equally well be included in this. On the other hand, if the Fungi are regarded as

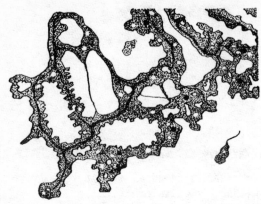

A.1   A slime mould (Myxomycetes) – fungus or colonial amoeba.

plants that have lost, in an evolutionary sense, their chlorophyll, the slime moulds belong to the kingdom Plantae. These strange organisms can therefore justifiably be included in four of the five kingdoms listed above. The only one to which they could not belong is the Monera, because they have cellulose cell walls like true plants and the cells contain nuclei.

There is no difficulty in deciding to what kingdom an evolutionarily advanced organism belongs. The problem arises at a lower level. Flagellates are often regarded as protozoan animals. Some, like the trypanosomes that are responsible for sleeping-sickness, are parasitic while others, such as the freshwater *Euglena*, contain chlorophyll, are free living and photosynthesise like plants. The distinction between them and unicellular algae lies in the fact that the latter possess cellulose cell walls. Classification ultimately depends upon the opinion of the taxonomist who decides which of many characters are the more important.

The organisms in the various kingdoms are divided into smaller groups or phyla. The Arthropoda is one phylum. Phyla are subdivided into smaller groups known as classes. Crustacea, Arachnida and Insecta are classes of the phylum Arthropoda. Classes, in turn, are divided into orders, orders into families and families into genera. The smallest major subdivision is the species. For example there are two species of camel, the one-humped dromedary and the two-humped bactrian camel. These both belong to the same genus *Camelus* and to the species *C.dromedarius* and *C.bactrianus* respectively.

APPENDIX II

Classification of world climates and vegetation

A   **Hot climates**: Mean annual temperatures above 21 °C.

     1 Equatorial   (Rainforest)
     2 Tropical marine   (Rainforest)
     3 Tropical continental   (Savanna)

B   **Warm temperate (or sub-tropical)**: No month below 6 °C.

     1 Western margin   (Temperate forest)
     2 Eastern margin   (Temperate forest)
     3 Continental   (Steppe)

C   **Cool temperate**: One to five months below 6 °C.

     1 Marine   (Temperate forest)
     2 Continental   (Taiga or steppe)

D   **Cold climates**: Six or more months below 6 °C.

     1 Marine   (Taiga)
     2 Continental or boreal   (Taiga or steppe)

E   **Arctic climates**: No month above 10 °C.

                                  (Tundra)

F   **Desert climates**: Low rainfall.

     1 Hot: No month below 6 °C
     2 Cold: One or more months below 6 °C

G   **Mountain climates**.

APPENDIX III

Simple statistical methods for estimating the size and analysing the distribution and density of populations

It is assumed that calculation of **standard deviation**, the t test of significance and the χ^2 test are familiar to readers with a knowledge of elementary statistics. The simplest and most direct method of finding out how many plants or animals are living in a particular area is of course to count them all. This can actually be done in the case of trees and large mammals etc., but is not possible for numerous smaller organisms whose populations have to be estimated from **samples** – except in the case of special habitats such as carcases, dung heaps, or under stones, planks etc. when every animal present can be counted.

Samples are assumed to be representative of the entire habitat from which they have been taken and the more samples there are the greater confidence there is in this assumption. It is also assumed that the population is either dispersed uniformly or randomly and that it is not clumped. More samples need to be studied if the dispersal is random than if it is uniform (and many more still if clumping is to be taken into account so that enough clumps are included for them to be included randomly).

In ecological studies samples are frequently obtained by means of **quadrats**. These are relatively small areas chosen at random from a larger area which contains the whole population. The quadrat grid is a rectangular frame made from metal or it can be pegged out with string on the ground. The plants or animals within it that belong to the populations to be studied are then counted. The size of the quadrat depends upon the size of the area to be sampled and numbers of the species to be investigated, but is usually 1 m² and divided into 8 or 16 (Figure A2). Often only one or two parts of the quadrat are used. Counting is carried out in numerous quadrats and the mean numbers assessed. The significance of the differences observed

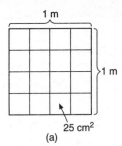

(a)

A.2(a) Metre square quadrat subdivided into 25 cm squares.

between populations in various quadrats can be calculated using the t or χ^2 test as appropriate. If the probability P of a calculated value of t or χ^2 is less than 0.05 (i.e. 19:1), the observed data depart significantly from the hypothesis that is being examined. If this hypothesis is that there is no association between two variables, it is known as a **null** hypothesis. Quadrats along **transects** can be used to determine whether or not populations are changing significantly. Quadrats situated at random may show no significant difference among the numbers of plants or animals within them, or may disclose aggregation.

Quadrats that have been subdivided can also be used to assess percentage cover by plant species. For instance, some quadrats might contain 10 per cent creeping buttercups (*Ranunculus repens*) and 40 per cent meadow buttercups (*R. acris* (Figure A2(b))), while the percentages are different in others. The significance of these differences could then be determined.

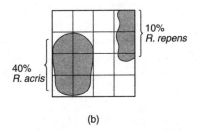

(b)

A.2(b) Estimation of percentage cover of different species of buttercup (*Ranunculus acris* and *R. repens*) within a quadrat.

In order to ensure that quadrats are selected randomly and without bias, grids are often thrown with the eyes shut. Alternatively, they may be sited according to a table of random numbers. When placed along the lines of a transect they can be used to determine zonation – for instance of barnacles across a rocky beach or of plant species in a wood (Figure A2(c)).

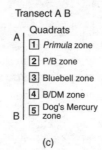

(c)

A.2(c) Transect of quadrats showing intergrading zones of primulas, bluebells, and dog's mercury.

Capture and recapture (The Petersen or Lincoln method). Several animals are captured and marked (by paint, toe clipping etc.) so that they can easily be recognised when caught a second time. Assuming 100 per cent survival in a **closed** population – that is, one that is not changing during the study period – the total population can be calculated as follows:

$$\frac{\text{Total number of individuals caught and marked}}{\text{THE TOTAL POPULATION (i.e. what we want to know)}} = \frac{\text{Total number of marked individuals recaught}}{\text{The total number recaught}}$$

therefore TOTAL POPULATION =

$$\frac{\text{Total number first caught and marked} \times \text{Total number caught on the second occasion}}{\text{Number of marked specimens in the second catch}}$$

Poisson distribution. Random distribution is described mathematically by the Poisson series in which the number of uniform samples selected at random containing 1, 2, 3, 4, 5, ... individuals conform to successive terms of the series.

$$s^2 = \frac{\Sigma\,(fx^2 - [\Sigma\,fx^2]\,/N]}{(N-1)}$$

where Σ = the sum of . . . ., f = frequency of . . . ., x = values of the numbers of animals per sample and N = number of samples. The probability (p) of finding a certain number (x) of animals from a population with a given mean ($\bar{x}$) and a Poisson distribution is given by:

$$px = e^{-\bar{x}}\,\frac{x^{-x}}{x!}$$

where e = roots of natural (**napierian**) logarithms, so that e^{-x} may be found using log tables. The goodness of fit of the data to Poisson distribution can be tested by χ^2 on the observed and expected values, or by the Index of dispersion.

Index of dispersion. This is the departure of the distribution of a population from randomness. It is sometimes referred to as the **coefficient of dispersal**. The extent to which the distribution satisfies a Poisson series can be tested by:

$$\chi^2 = \frac{s^2\,(N-1)}{\bar{x}}$$

where s^2 = variance, N number of samples and $\bar{x}$ = the mean. If the distribution is indeed Poisson, the χ^2 value calculated will not lie outside the limits (0.95 and 0.05) of χ^2 for $N-1$ in the tables. If the χ^2 does conform with Poisson expectation, the index of dispersion = $\chi^2\,/\,(N-1)$ and will approximate to unity. A value of 0 for the index will imply that the animals were uniformly distributed and a value significantly greater than 1.0 implies aggregation.

Morisita's standardized index (lp) can also be used to determine the patterns of dispersion. $1p = 0.5 + 0.5\,[(ld - Mc)/(n-Mc)]$ where l^d is the index of dispersion, n = sample size, and Mc = clumped index. The Morisita index is one of the best measures of dispersion because it is independent of density and sample size. If $lp = 0$, the population sample has a random pattern of dispersal. If $lp < 0$, it shows a uniform pattern and if $lp > 0$, the pattern is clumped.

Many other tests of dispersal have been devised.

Index of similarity between floristic **provinces** and **tension zones** is sometimes a useful measurement for deciding whether two habitats have identical vegetation or not. It is calculated as follows:

$$\frac{2c}{(x + y)}$$

where x is the number of species in one community, y is the number in the second and c is the number common to both. The index ranges from 0 to 1.0.

For practical examples see: Southwood, T.R.E. *Ecological Methods. With particular reference to the study of insect populations* (2nd Edn), London: Chapman & Hall (1978), Chambers, E.G. *Statistical Calculation for Beginners* (2nd Edn), Cambridge: Cambridge University Press (1952), or another elementary text book on statistics.

APPENDIX IV

Intensities and dates of the five major mass extinctions in the fossil record

(Simplified from D. Jablonski)

	Percentage of observed loss of families	Percentage of calculated species loss	Million years ago
Ordovician	26	84	438
Devonian	22	79	360
Permian	51	95	248
Triassic	22	79	213
Cretaceous	16	70	65

BIBLIOGRAPHY

A wide selection of books on ecological topics is presented in order to illustrate their range and diversity.

General ecology

Cockburn, A. (1991) *An Introduction to Evolutionary Ecology*. Oxford: Blackwell.

Colinvaux, P. (1993) *Ecology*, 2. New York: Wiley.

Dajoz, R. (1977) *Introduction to Ecology*. London: Hodder & Stoughton.

Dowdeswell, W.H. (1984) *Ecology. Principles and practice*. London: Heinemann.

Howe, H.F. & Westley, L.C. (1988) *Ecological Relationships of Plants and Animals*. Oxford: Oxford University Press.

Knight, C.B. (1965) *Basic Concepts of Ecology*. New York: Macmillan.

Kormandy, E.J. (1996) *Concepts of Ecology* (4th Edn). New Jersey: Prentice Hall.

Krebs, C.J. (1972) *Ecology. The experimental analysis of distribution and abundance*. New York: Harper & Row.

Odum, E.P. (1959) *Fundamentals of Ecology* (2nd Edn). Philadelphia: W.B. Saunders.

Owen, D.F. (1974) *What is Ecology?* London: Oxford University Press.

Peters, R.H. (1991) *A Critique for Ecology*. Cambridge: Cambridge University Press.

Pianka, E.R. (1994) *Evolutionary Ecology* (5th Edn). New York: Harper Collins.

Putnam, R.J. (1994) *Community Ecology*. London: Chapman & Hall.

Remmert, H. (1880) *Ecology. A textbook*. Berlin: Springer.

Ricklefs, R.E. (1990) *Ecology* (3rd Edn). New York: W.H. Freeman.

Ricklefs, R.E. (1997) *The Economy of Nature* (4th Edn). New York: W.H. Freeman.

Roughgarden, J., May, R.M. & Lewis S.A. (Eds) (1989) *Perspectives in Ecological Theory*. Princeton, NJ: Princeton University Press.

Scott, M. (1994) *Ecology* (Young Oxford Books). Oxford: Oxford University Press.

Smith, R.L. (1996) *Ecology and Field Biology* (5th Edn). New York: Harper Collins.

Stiling, P.D. (1996) *Ecology. Theories and application* (2nd Edn). New Jersey: Prentice Hall.

Stonehouse, B. & Perrins, C.M. (Eds) (1977) *Evolutionary Ecology*. London: Macmillan.

Animal ecology

Allee, W.C., Emerson, A.E., Park, O., Park, T. & Schmidt, K.P. (1949) *Principles of Animal Ecology*. Philadelphia: W.B.Saunders.

Chapman, R.N. (1931) *Animal Ecology. With especial reference to insects*. New York: McGraw-Hill.

Elton, C.S. (1927) *Animal Ecology*. London: Sidgwick & Jackson.

Elton, C.S. (1966) *The Pattern of Animal Communities*. London: Methuen.

Macfadyen, A. (1963) *Animal Ecology. Aims and methods*. London: Sir Isaac Pitman & Sons.

Plant ecology

Bormann, P.H. & Likens, G.E. (1979) *Pattern and Process in a Forested Ecosystem*. New York: Springer.

Boulier, R. (Ed.) (1983) *Tropical Savannas*. Amsterdam: Elsevier.

Braun-Blanquet, J. (1965) *Plant Sociology. The study of plant communities* (Revised transl). New York: Hafner.

Crawford, R.M.M. (1989) *Studies in Plant Survival*. Oxford: Blackwell.

Frity, B. & Legrand, M. (Eds) (1993) *Mechanisms of Plant Defense Responses* (Developments in Plant Pathology). Dordrecht: Kluwer.

Grieg-Smith, P. (1964) *Quantitative Plant Ecology* (2nd Edn). London: Butterworth.

Oosteng, H.J. (1950) *The Study of Plant Communities*. San Francisco: W.H. Freeman.

Ovington, J.D. (1983) *Temperate Broad-leaved Evergreen Forests*. Amsterdam: Elsevier.

Tansley, A.G. (1939) *The British Isles and their Vegetation* (2 vols). Cambridge: Cambridge University Press.

Walter, H. (1973) *Vegetation of the Earth. In relation to climate and the eco-physiological conditions*. Berlin: Springer.

Walter, H. & Breckle, S-W. (1985) *Ecological Systems of the Geobiosphere 1. Ecological principles in global perspective*. Berlin: Springer.

Willis, A.J. (1973) *Introduction to Plant Ecology*. London: Allen & Unwin.

Woodward, F.I. (1987) *Climate and Plant Distribution*. Cambridge: Cambridge University Press.

Population ecology

Andrewartha, H.G. (1961) *Introduction to the Study of Animal Populations*. London: Methuen.

Andrewartha, H.G. & Birch, L.C. (1954) *The Distribution and Abundance of Animals*. Chicago: Chicago University Press.

Begon, M., Harper, J.L. & Townsend, C.R. (1990) *Ecology. Individuals, populations and communities* (2nd Edn). Boston: Blackwell.

Berryman, A.A. (1981) *Population Systems. A general introduction*. New York: Plenum Press.

Cody, M.L. & Diamond, J.M. (Eds) (1975). *Ecology and Evolution of Communities*. Cambridge, MA: Harvard University Press.

Cohen, J. (1978) *Food Webs and Niche Space*. Princeton, NJ: Princeton University Press.

Crawley, M.J. (Ed.) (1992) *Natural Enemies. The population biology of predators, parasites and disease*. Oxford: Blackwell.

Hutchinson, G.E. (1978) *An Introduction to Population Ecology*. New Haven: Yale University Press.

Krebs, C.J. (1994) *Ecology. The experimental analysis of distribution and abundance* (4th Edn). New York: Harper Collins.

Lack, D. (1954) *The Natural Regulation of Animal Numbers*. London: Oxford University Press.

Lack, D. (1966). *Population Studies of Birds*. Oxford: Clarendon Press.

Polis, G.A. & Winemiller, K.O. (Eds) (1996) *Food Webs. Integration of patterns and dynamics*. New York: Chapman & Hall.

Putman, R.J. (1994) *Community Ecology*. London: Chapman & Hall.

Southwood, T.R.E. (1978) *Ecological Methods. With particular reference to the study of insect populations* (2nd Edn). London: Chapman & Hall.

Tanner, J.T. (1978) *Guide to the Study of Animal Populations*. Knoxville: University of Tennessee Press.

Wynne-Edwards, V.C. (1962) *Animal Dispersion in Relation to Social Behaviour*. Edinburgh: Oliver & Boyd.

Marine ecology

Barnes, B. (1986) *Guide to Coast and Shore* (British Naturalists' Association). Marlborough, Wilts: Crowood Press.

Barnes, R.S.K. (1974) *Estuarine Biology* (Institute of Biology, Studies in Biology, No.49). London: Edward Arnold.

Hardy, A.C. (1956) *The Open Sea* 1: *The world of plankton*. (The New Naturalist). London: Collins.

Hardy, A.C. (1959) *The Open Sea*. II: *Fish and fisheries* (The New Naturalist). London: Collins.

Lewis, J.R. (1964) *The Ecology of Rocky Shores*. London: English Universities Press.

McLusky, D. (1989) *The Estuarine Ecosystem* (2nd Edn). New York: Chapman & Hall.

Russell, F.S. & Yonge, C.M. (1936) *The Seas. Our knowledge of life in the seas and how it is gained* (2nd Edn). London: Frederick Warne.

Thorson, G. (1971) *Life in the Sea* (Transl. M.C. Meilgaard & A.Laurie). London: Weidenfeld and Nicolson.

Yonge, C.M. (1949) *The Sea Shore* (The New Naturalist). London: Collins.

Freshwater ecology

Barnes, E.K. & Mann, K.H. (Eds) (1980) *Fundamentals of Aquatic Ecosystems*. Oxford: Blackwell.

Carpenter, K.E. (1928) *Life in Inland Waters with especial reference to animals*. London: Sidgwick & Jackson.

Clegg, J. (1985) *Guide to Ponds and Streams* (British Naturalists' Association). Marlborough, Wilts.: Crowood Press.

Leadley-Brown, A. (1971) *Ecology of Fresh Water*. London: Heinemann Educational.

Macan, T.T. (1966) *Freshwater Ecology*. London: Longman.

Macan, T.T. (1973) *Ponds and Lakes*. London: Allen & Unwin.

Macan, T.T. & Worthington, E.B. (1951) *Life in Lakes and Rivers* (The New Naturalist). London: Collins.

Terrestrial ecology

Brookes, B. (1985) *Guide to Mountain and Moorland*. (British Naturalists' Association). Marlborough, Wilts.: Crowood Press.

Chapman, P. (1993) *Caves and Cave Life* (The New Naturalist). London: Harper Collins.

Cloudsley-Thompson, J.L. (1967) *Microecology* (Institute of Biology, Studies in Biology, No.6). London: Edward Arnold.

Cloudsley-Thompson, J.L. (1975) *Terrestrial Environments*. London: Croom Helm.

Cloudsley-Thompson, J.L. (Ed.) (1984) *Sahara Desert* (Key Environments). Oxford: Pergamon Press.

Cloudsley-Thompson, J.L. (1985) *Guide to Woodlands* (British Naturalists' Association). Marlborough, Wilts.: Crowood Press.

Cloudsley-Thompson, J.L. (1996) *Biotic Interactions in Arid Lands* (Adaptations of Desert Organisms). Berlin: Springer.

Coupland, R.T. (Ed.) (1992) *Natural Grasslands* (Ecosystems of the World) (2 Vols). Amsterdam: Elsevier.

Culver, D.C. (1982) *Cave Life. Evolution and ecology*. Cambridge, MA: Harvard University Press.

Darling, F.F. & Boyd, J.M. (1947) *The Highlands and Islands* (The New Naturalist). London: Collins.

Freethy, R. (1986) *Guide to Wildlife in Towns* (British Naturalists' Association). Marlborough, Wilts.: Crowood Press.

Gimmingham, C.H. (1972) *Ecology of Heathlands*. London: Chapman & Hall.

Gimmingham, C.H. (1975) *An Introduction to Heathland Ecology*. Edinburgh: Oliver & Boyd.

Goodall, D.W., Perry, R.A. & Howes, K.M.W. (Eds) (1979) *Arid-land Ecosystems: Structure, functioning and management*, Vol.1. Cambridge: Cambridge University Press.

Goodall, D.W., Perry, R.A. & Howes, K.M.W. (Eds) (1981) *Arid-land Ecosystems: Structure, functioning and management*, Vol.2. Cambridge: Cambridge University Press.

Jacobs, M. & Oldeman, A.A. (1987) *The Tropical Rain Forest: a first encounter*. New York: Springer.

Lee, B. (1985) *Guide to Fields, Farms and Hedgerows* (British Naturalists' Association). Marlborough, Wilts.: Crowood Press.

Miles, P.M. & Miles, H.B. (1968) *Chalkland and Moorland Ecology*. London: Hulton.

Pearsall, W.H. (1950) *Mountains and Moorlands* (The New Naturalist). London: Collins.

Polis, G.A. (Ed.) (1991) *The Ecology of Desert Communities*. Tucson: University of Arizona Press.

Richards, P.W. (1952) *The Tropical Rainforest*. Cambridge: Cambridge University Press.

Rundel, P.W. & Gibson, A.C. (1996) *Ecological Communities and Processes in a Mojave Desert Ecosystem: Rock Valley, Nevada*. Cambridge: Cambridge University Press.

Sankey, J.H.P. (1958) *A Guide to Field Biology*. London: Longmans, Green.

Sankey, J. (1966) *Chalkland Ecology*. London: Heinemann Educational Books.

Shelford, V.E. (1963) *The Ecology of North America*. Urbana: University of Illinois Press.

Unwin, D.M. (1980) *Microclimate Measurements for Ecologists*. London: Academic Press.

Vandel, A. (1965) *Biospeleology. The biology of cavernicolous animals* (Transl. B.E. Freeman). Oxford: Pergamon Press.

Soils

Brady, N.C. (1974) *Nature and Property of Soils* (8th Edn). New York: Macmillan.

Bridges, E.M. (1970) *World Soils*. Cambridge: Cambridge University Press.

Eyre, S.R. (1963) *Vegetation and Soils: a world picture*. Chicago: Aldine.

Fitzpatrick, E.A. (1980) *Soils. Their formation, classification and distribution*. London: Longman.

Griffin, D.R. (1972) *Ecology of Soil Fungi*. London: Chapman & Hall.

Jenny, H. (1980) *The Soil Resource: origin and behavior*. New York: Springer.

Kühnelt, W. (1961) *Soil Biology with special reference to the animal kingdom*. (Transl. N.Walker). London: Faber and Faber.

Russell, E.J. (1957) *The World of the Soil* (The New Naturalist). London: Collins.

Wallwork, J.A. (1970) *The Ecology of Soil Animals*. London: McGraw-Hill.

Wallwork, J.A. (1976) *The Distribution and Diversity of Soil Fauna*. London: Academic Press.

Ecology of parasites

Chandler, A.C. & Read, C.P. (1961) *Introduction to Parasitology with special reference to the parasites of man* (10th Edn). New York: John Wiley and Sons.

Chang, T.C. (1986) *General Parasitology* (2nd Edn). Orlando: Academic Press.

Kennedy, C.R. (Ed.) (1976) *Ecological Aspects of Parasitology*. Amsterdam: North Holland.

Lane, R.P. & Crosskey, R.W. (Eds) (1993) *Medical Insects and Arachnids*. London: Chapman & Hall.

Rollinson, D. & Anderson, R.M. (Eds) (1985) *Ecology and Genetics of Host–Parasite Interactions*. London: Academic Press.

Rothschild, M. & Clay, T. (1952) *Fleas, Flukes & Cuckoos. A study of bird parasites* (The New Naturalist). London: Collins.

Conservation ecology

Jordan, C.F. (1985) *Nutrient Cycling in Tropical Rainforest Ecosystems: Principles and their application in management and conservation*. New York: John Wiley and Sons.

Southwick, C.H. (Ed.) (1985) *Global Ecology*. Sunderland, MA: Sinauer.

Spellerberg, I.F. (Ed.) (1996) *Conservation Biology*. Harlow, Essex: Longman.

General reading

Applin, D. (1997) *Key Science: Biology* (New Edn). Cheltenham: Stanley Thornes.

Baker, R.R. (1978) *The Evolutionary Ecology of Animal Migration*. Sevenoaks, Kent: Hodder & Stoughton.

Cloudsley-Thompson, J.L. (1978) *Animal Migration*. London: Orbis Publishing.

Cloudsley-Thompson, J.L. (1980) *Biological Clocks. Their functions in nature*. London: Weidenfeld and Nicolson.

Crawley, M.J. (1983) *Herbivory. The dynamics of animal-plant interactions*. Berkeley: University of California Press.

Elgar, M.A. & Crespi, B.J. (Eds) (1992) *Cannibalism. Ecology and evolution among diverse taxa*. Oxford: Oxford University Press.

Elton, C.S. (1958) *The Ecology of Invasions by Animals and Plants*. London: Methuen.

Evans, D.L. & Schmidt, E.O. (1990) *Insect Defenses. Adaption mechanisms and strategies of prey and predators*. Albany: State University of New York Press.

George, W. (1962) *Animal Geography*. London: Heinemann.

Gleick, J. (1988) *Chaos. Making a new science*. London: Cardinal.

Lotka, A.J. (1925) *Elements of Physical Biology*. Baltimore: Williams and Wilkins.

Lovelock, J.E. (1979) *Gaia*. Cambridge: Cambridge University Press.

Lovelock, J.E. (1988) *The Ages of Gaia*. Cambridge: Cambridge University Press

MacArthur, R.H. & Wilson, E.O. (1967) *The Theory of Island Biogeography*. Princeton, New Jersey: Princeton University Press.

Phillipson, J. (1966) *Ecological Energetics*. London: Edward Arnold.

Sprent, J.I. (1987) *The Ecology of the Nitrogen Cycle*. Cambridge: Cambridge University Press.

Thurman, E.M. (1955) *Organic Chemistry of Natural Waters*. Boston: Martinus Nyhoff/Dr W. Junk.

INDEX

Terms are usually defined when first mentioned